D1266560

2/18/63

THE CORPORATE REVOLUTION
IN AMERICA

The Corporate Revolution
In America

Economic Reality vs. Economic Theory

GARDINER C. MEANS

THE CROWELL-COLLIER PRESS

First Crowell-Collier Press Edition 1962

Library of Congress Catalog Card Number: 62-15809

Preface

THIS BOOK CONTAINS a collection of essays on the subject of big business and administered prices. Most of them first appeared as testimony before Congressional committees or as lectures before audiences in the United States and in Europe. Each is concerned with some aspect of the problem created by big business. Some are focused on the facts of bigness and of price administration; some are primarily concerned with the implications of these facts for economic theory; and some are more concerned with their implications for public policy.

My first awareness of the problem of bigness and its significance is reflected in the thesis which I submitted for a doctor's degree in 1933. This was entitled "The Corporate Revolution." It not only presented the facts which make the modern corporation so important and so different from the smaller enterprises of traditional experience, but also pointed to some of the basic implications of the modern corporation. The factual part of this thesis was accepted for the doctor's degree but the section on implications was rejected on the quite understandable ground that it was insufficiently developed. Fortunately the official summary of the dissertation covers both the facts and the suggested implications. It is reproduced as Chapter 1 of this book since the factual section provides essential background for the other essays, and the rejected section provided the challenge which ultimately led to the more extended development presented here.

The essays also include the section of a memorandum to the Secretary of Agriculture in 1934 which first introduced the concept of an administered price and gave the factual substance to support its importance.

Other essays had their genesis in lectures delivered at the College of William and Mary, Carleton College and the Ohio State Law School in the United States; in lectures to the fellows of the American Seminar in Salzburg, to labor officials in Vienna, and to economists and students in Belgrade and other cities of Yugoslavia; and in testimony presented to three different Congressional committees.

The essays fall naturally into two groups. The essay introducing the corporate revolution and that introducing administered prices combine with the essay on the Roosevelt Revolution to set the stage. The remaining essays, all developed in the last five years, are concerned with the implication of the revolution for economic theory and for current government policy.

Because of the wide variety of audiences to which the materials were addressed, they involve a considerable amount of repetition. In order to discuss a particular aspect of the larger problem with the particular audience it was often necessary to present the same set of underlying ideas. To some extent, repetition has been reduced in editing the essays. But in many cases it has seemed best to include the repetition of theme in order to maintain the rhythm of the particular essay.

While this book is concerned only with developments in the United States, the modern corporation and administered prices have come to play an increasing role in other highly industrialized countries. Canada, England, Germany and Japan are outstanding in this respect. Each of these countries is finding itself faced with essentially the same set of basic problems. Thus, while in detail this volume is concerned only with the corporate revolution in America, it in some degree mirrors the corporate revolution which is taking place in the major industrial countries of the free world. It is this revolution which is undercutting so fundamentally the basis of Communism—the Marxian theory.

GARDINER C. MEANS

December 16, 1961

ACKNOWLEDGMENTS

Acknowledgment is due to *Science* and to the *Harvard Business Review* for permission to republish the essay on "Collective Capitalism and Economic Theory"; to Anderson Kramer Associates for permission to republish the essay on "Administrative Inflation and Public Policy"; to Bram Cavin, the Collier Books editor who originated the idea of publishing these essays; to Miss Margaret V. Means who assisted in the editing; and to my publishers, Harper and Brothers, for their liberal interpretation of our contract which permits this volume of earlier writings to be published independently.

CONTENTS

CHAPTER ONE

The Corporate Revolution

The following essay appeared under the title, "The Corporate Revolution," in the Summaries of PhD Theses— *1933, Harvard University. The factual material summarized here appeared in* The Modern Corporation and Private Property *written jointly with Adolf A. Berle, Jr. (New York: The Macmillan Co., 1933) and has become a part of the accepted image of the modern economy. The section on theoretical implications suggests the profound rethinking of theory and policy which the corporate revolution makes necessary and which the remaining essays elaborate.*

THIS THESIS PRESENTS statistical evidence of a change in the fundamental character of economic organization which has been brought about through the growth of corporate activity, and attempts to indicate certain of the more important changes in the assumptions of economic analysis which this development requires. It is suggested that this development, culminating in the separation of ownership and control, has brought a change in the character of industry as revolutionary as that produced by the industrial revolution with its corresponding division of function, the separation of labor and control.

The statistical part of the thesis shows (1) the increasing extent to which economic activity is conducted under the corporate form of organization, (2) the increasing role which corporations of tremendous size have come to play, (3) the increasing dispersion of stock ownership, and finally (4) the increasing separation of ownership and control which is involved in the modern corporation.

The theoretical section takes four major postulates of received economic theory—the trading character of the market, the determinacy of cost, the unity of the process of real saving, and the efficacy of the profit motive—and suggests that modern corporate enterprise makes it necessary to replace these, in so far as corporate enterprise is concerned, with (1) the administrative character of the market, (2) the indeterminacy of cost, (3) the duality of the process of saving, and finally (4) the possible ineffectiveness of "profits" as a motivating force.

Following an introduction, the thesis sketches the development of corporate economic activity in the United States from the 335 corporations of 1800 to the half million corporations of the present day. It is shown that the corporation has come to dominate field after field of business enterprise, coming earliest in those fields invested with a public interest (banks, insurance companies, and common carriers), or in those requiring large aggregate fixed capital (railroads or mines); latest in those involving little public interest (public services, agriculture, etc.), and in those requiring little fixed capital (wholesale and retail trade). The trend of the last century indicates that in the very near future virtually all economic enterprise will be conducted by corporations with the possible important exception of farming.

The thesis then indicates that in the growth of corporate enterprise very large corporations have come to be the dominant form. In 1927, two hundred non-financial corporations controlled 45 percent of non-financial corporate wealth, received over 40 percent of corporate income, controlled 35 percent of business wealth, and between 15 and 20 percent of national wealth. The rate of growth of large corporations between 1909 and 1927 has been such that if it were to continue 80 percent of corporate wealth would be in the hands of two hundred corporations by 1950.[1]

The thesis also shows the growth in the number of book stockholders in recent years for three of the largest corporations in the country, for thirty-one representative big companies, and for all corporations (estimated). The latter increased from 4.4 million in 1900 to 12 million in 1920 and 18 million in 1928. Customer and employee stock ownership is considered and a shift of ownership from the rich to the less well-to-do is shown from income tax statistics.

The statistical section of the thesis examines the separation of ownership and control in the large corporations in the United States. Five types of control are considered: complete ownership; majority control; control through a legal device; minority control; and management control. Examination of the ultimate control of the two hundred largest American corporations indicates these striking facts: 65 percent of them by number and 80 percent by assets are controlled by management or by a legal device under which ownership and control are separated; 23 percent by number and 14 percent by assets represent control by minority ownership. This leaves 12 percent by number and 6 percent by assets which are actually controlled by majority of the ownership. It is suggested that this corporate development calls for a re-analysis of the economic process in which the individualism of Adam Smith's private

[1] It should be noted that this statement was not a prediction but an indication of the magnitude of the rate at which growth was proceeding in the twenty-year period. Concentration did continue after 1929 but at a much slower rate. Government action under the Roosevelt and subsequent administrations has operated to slow the rate of concentration, breaking up utility holding companies, impeding railroad consolidation, preventing industrial mergers and, in the case of aluminum, eliminating monopoly by facilitating the creation of effective competitors.

enterprise has given way to the collective activity of the modern corporation.

The theoretical section examines the central core of received theory as it was developed by Adam Smith and given greater precision by later writers. The received theory can be summarized as the application of the principle of substitution to both the factors of production and the means of consumption, under the assumption of markets for both in which supply is equated to demand through a perfectly flexible price. It assumes what might properly be called a trading market. Earlier writers have recognized that economic activity is only in part trading and that the element of administration enters in, but they have tended to minimize this administrative aspect. The modern corporation has not only increased this aspect by bringing a greater part of economic activity within the administrative limits of single units, but has altered the character of the market by making *price* not an outgrowth of trading but of administration. Prices fixed over periods of time have replaced flexible prices, and supply as defined by classical economists is seldom equated to demand. Rather, *production* tends to be equated to demand at the fixed prices and a disequilibrium between *supply* and demand results not in a fall in price, but in the failure fully to employ the factors of production, or in their over-employment.

The next section suggests that as all enterprise activity involves "overhead costs" and as these are essentially "joint costs," it would be more precise to assume that every product of enterprise activity is a product of joint cost and, correspondingly, that every product involves joint utility. The importance of the organized relationship of items of wealth in the modern corporation makes this assumption essential. Under this assumption both cost and utility become indeterminate.

It is then suggested that the process of saving has come

to be a dual process conducted by two independent groups of individuals, whose actions do not necessarily mesh, with the result that two separate and independent markets exist, one for capital goods and one for interests in capital goods. It is indicated that prices in these markets may move in opposite directions or in the same direction.

Finally the thesis indicates that where ownership and control are completely separated and profits are destined only for the "owners" they cannot perform their customary role of inducing the efficient management of enterprise, though they can perform the role of inducing the taking of risk. It is suggested that if the logic of traditional profit theory were to be followed, any profits over and above enough given to the "owners" to induce the continued supply of new capital should be received by control as a prize to induce the efficient management of enterprise. Because such great profits to control would presumably involve diminishing returns, the question is raised whether profits are a socially effective method of inducing enterprise activity [where the modern corporation is concerned].

CHAPTER TWO

The Roosevelt Revolution and The New Reality

This chapter was first given in 1960 as a Convocation Address at Carleton College, the old home of Thorstein Veblen. It stresses the basic shift in government policy which was forced by the reality of the corporate revolution and the exigencies of the Great Depression of the 1930's.

IT IS NOW more than three decades since Black Thursday on the stock exchange ushered in the three years of economic decline which culminated in the collapse of the banking system and the virtual breakdown of the free enterprise system itself. I will here be concerned with the New Deal, which re-established the free enterprise system as a going concern.

At this distance it is often difficult to appreciate the extent of the economic collapse and the great re-establishment which occurred after Roosevelt came to power in March of 1933. Walter Lippmann did not exaggerate when he said in late 1933, "At the end of February we were a congeries of disorderly panic-stricken mobs and factions. In the hundred days from March to June we became again an organized nation confident of our power to provide for our own security and to control our own destiny."

I am going to speak of this transformation as the Roosevelt Revolution. This is the term which was applied in the summer of 1933 when the legislative program of that year was completed and so many of the major principles of the New Deal were established. But then, as business began to pick up and it became apparent that the New Deal was reestablishing the free enterprise system it became popular to say, "This is no revolution."

Actually it was a great revolution—a revolution in point of view. This country had backed into the twentieth century, describing its economy in terms of Adam Smith's small enterprise and Alfred Marshall's small representative firm. The theories and clichés which constituted our inherited wisdom and which we relied on to guide public policy were developed for an atomistic society which had in large measure ceased to exist. For more than a century this inherited wisdom had served to guide policy toward the effective operation of our free enterprise system. But in 1932 the system was approaching collapse and national policies based on this inherited wisdom were not halting the collapse. The revolution which Roosevelt made was to turn away from this classical wisdom and look directly at the potentials of our modern big-business economy.

This about-face from classical theory to the modern potentials was a profound revolution. It did not reject the theory or practice of democracy. It did not reject the theory or practice of free enterprise. What it did do was to reject classical economic theory as the basis for operating the free enterprise system.

On the other hand, it did not substitute an alternative, ready-made theory for making a modern free enterprise system work. There was no such theory. Neither the theories of communism and socialism nor those of fascism gave any guide for a democratic society. The approach was and had to be pragmatic.

The pragmatic character of New Deal policy is often hard to keep in mind. A student recently came to discuss his doctor's thesis with me. His subject was "The Theory of the New Deal," and it soon became apparent that he really meant *the* theory. I am afraid that I laughed as I explained that there was no single New Deal theory. Undoubtedly there were pieces of theories, but no single theory, and all theory was suspect.

We can liken the New Deal situation to that of a Mexican Indian I once photographed. He was not used to seeing pictures and when I showed him the photograph of himself it simply did not register. All he could see was patches of black and grey and white. I explained to him that it was a picture of himself, that he was facing that way, there was his head, and there were his feet. And finally the picture came into focus. In an analogous way the New Deal revolution brought our actual economy into view in place of the nineteenth-century model. It opened up new frontiers and new unexplored potentials. But until the new potentials were brought into focus and their implications were clear, pragmatic action and exploration were the only possible actions. I used to say that if our society could get a clear view of its economic self within a fifteen-year period, this would be fast work.

Let me elaborate this because I believe it is fundamental to our understanding of the Roosevelt Revolution.

First, I want to mention the relation between theory and reality. Any complex theory, whether it be classical physics or classical economics, is rigidly tied to its basic assumptions. Newton's basic assumptions of mass and motion in a sense imprisoned his theory. Classical physics could elaborate the implications of these basic assumptions, but within their framework the reality of the Michaelson-Morley experiment or the bending of light by the sun could not be explained. Only a revision of the basic assumption could provide the modern physics of quantum and relativity. Economic theory is imprisoned in the same way. When you adopt the basic classical assumptions of very small enterprise, a large number of buyers and sellers, and prices determined by supply and demand, the scope of your theory is limited by these assumptions. However much you elaborate your theory, you cannot explain real behavior which lies outside the prison of these assumptions.

It is for this reason that I want to liken social theory to a straight line and social reality to a curve. The social reality is constantly changing. The feudal system gave way to the private enterprise system and that has been giving way to the corporate enterprise system. This is the curve of social reality. But a social theory like mercantilism or classical economics, because it cannot change beyond the limits of its own basic assumptions, has to travel in a straight line.

A good social theory, such as classical economic theory, is one which closely fits the reality of a given time. We can say that it is a line tangent to the curve of reality. In this sense the classical theory was clearly tangent to the reality of the nineteenth century, and while a social theory is tangent to reality it can be an effective guide to social policy. Social actions taken in terms of the theory produce pretty much the results to be expected from theory.

But then as the social reality changes, the line of theory gets further and further from the curve of reality. Discrepancies develop between the result of policy based on the theory and those to be expected from the theory. Tensions develop and controversy rages. Conflicting theories strive to gain allegiance. Ultimately a new theory crystallizes and gains acceptance which is more nearly tangent to the new reality, and society is again squared away for a period in which social policy produces pretty much the results that theory predicts.

But the period between the rejection of the old theory and the development and general acceptance of the new is necessarily a period of confusion, of trial and error, of experimentation. In my opinion the six years of the New Deal were just such a period. Not only did the leaders of the New Deal recognize that the old policies were not producing the results to be expected—recovery was still hiding around the corner—but the invalidity of two of the basic assumptions of classical theory was increasingly recognized. It was recognized that the modern economy was not an economy of small enterprise but that its dominant characteristic was big enterprise. Presumably this is why the book Adolf Berle and I wrote, *The Modern Corporation and Private Property,* was sometimes called the bible of the New Deal. Also, it was recognized that the pricing process was significantly different from that assumed in classical theory. In large areas of the economy, prices were not and could not be determined by market forces but were administered and tended to be relatively insensitive to changes in demand and costs. Competition among the few did not produce the same results as competition among the many. And both of these characteristics of modern reality were in conflict with the classical assumptions.

You may suggest, as others have, that the giants of classical theory were perfectly aware of big business and administered prices. And I will agree with you. But that is not the question. The question is whether they built these characteristics of an economy into their theory. Did the classical model contain big business and administered prices? I say No and will give two concrete examples to establish this point.

First consider Alfred Marshall, the greatest of the classical economists. In his *Principles* he built his analysis on the representative firm, a relatively small firm with a short life cycle of growth and decay. He thought of each industry as consisting of hundreds or even thousands of such firms. In his famous analogy, he likened an industry to a forest with individual trees sprouting, growing and finally declining, with the whole maintained as new trees replaced the old. In his own words, "As with the growth of trees, so it is with the growth of business." This is what he wrote in 1890 and this is the conception around which his theory is built. He did not try to introduce the big modern corporation into his analysis. Indeed in his sixth edition published in 1910 he virtually said as much when he changed the sentence I have quoted to read, "As with the growth of trees, so it *was* with the growth of business as a general rule before the recent development of vast joint-stock companies." But his *Principles* were never revised to take account of this momentous change.

Or take Leon Walras' famous system of equations. This set of equations is justifiably regarded as the epitome of classical theory. And yet if one introduces a single administered price into the system, the equations cannot be solved. A single administered price shatters the system as effectively as a monkey wrench thrown into a complex machine. How can such a theory provide a guide to policy when the majority of prices are administered? I think we can say without hesitation that classical theory and its wisdom were not about an economy in which big business, few competitors and administered prices play a major role.

This does not mean that classical theory was wrong. For more than a century it had served well to guide policy. It was closely tangent to the reality of that time. As long as enterprises were predominantly small and the great bulk of prices were determined by market forces, the wisdom derived from classical theory could provide constructive policy. Expressed in such clichés as "laissez-faire," "that government governs best which governs least," "balance the budget," "sound money," and "maintain business confidence," it could and did allow this country a tremendous expansion.

Let us look at what this body of theory offered.

First, it said that, if its policies were followed, the unseen hand of market forces would automatically provide full employment. Say's law said there could not be general over-production or under-consumption. The only condition of equilibrium was one of full employment and any temporary departure from equilibrium would tend to be quickly corrected. The free enterprise economy was a cybernetic mechanism automatically tending to full employment. In any recession recovery was just around the corner if the government would just keep its hands off and not interfere.

Second, classical theory said that the market mechanism would so adjust prices as to direct resources of manpower and capital into the most effective uses. For a small-business, free-enterprise system, I believe this would be substantially true except for the exploitation of natural resources.

Third, classical theory said the market mechanism would so adjust prices as to reward the factors of production in proportion to their contribution. This also I accept as at least a first approximation to the truth for a free small enterprise system.

According to classical theory, if individuals were out of work or received low incomes it was because they were lazy or inefficient workers. It was their own fault. If recession appeared, it was due to friction in the system and the main role of government was to maintain business confidence and not rock the boat. If business exploitation was wasting natural resources it was the product of miscalculation which better information would correct.

At the time of our near collapse, government policy was in the hands of strong protagonists of the classical wisdom and the policies prescribed by that wisdom were in the main being followed and were proving a failure.

It is true that certain significant departures from traditional wisdom were made by the old deal. Under the leadership of Governor Strong of the New York Federal Reserve Bank, New York bankers attempted a rather naïve form of monetary management. As this failed and the Great Depression gathered momentum, Hoover called in the heads of big business and persuaded them to adopt a policy of maintaining current wage rates—a policy in direct conflict with the classical wisdom. And, as business failures increased, Hoover set up the Reconstruction Finance Corporation to keep big businesses from going to pieces. Both of these actions were in tune with the reality of modern enterprise and each was directed against the automatic correctives of classical theory. Yet it is because, in the main, the classical automatic correctives were relied on for recovery that these minor and realistic departures from classical wisdom had such little success. They do, however, help to underline the discrepancy between the straight line of classical theory and the curve of economic reality.

When Roosevelt came to power he made the great revolution. He turned his back on the classical wisdom. This is the fundamental reform which he made. He rejected the theory that the modern free enterprise system would automatically tend to maintain full employment, he rejected the theory that the unemployed were responsible for their own unemployment, and he rejected the theory that incomes reached through the market system tended to reflect the individual's contribution to production.

This about-face opened up new frontiers of positive action by government to make the modern free enterprise system a success. I think this is what Winston Churchill meant when he said in 1934, "For in truth, Roosevelt is an explorer who has embarked on a voyage as uncertain as that of Columbus, and upon a quest which might conceivably be as important as the discovery of the New World."

Let us look, then, at Roosevelt's initial program as laid down in the first hundred days.

Probably the most basic single reform was that of the monetary system and the establishment of monetary management by government. To this end, bank deposits were guaranteed; gold was drawn from the bankers and the public into the hands of government; monetary banking was separated from investment banking; money in the economy was released from rigid internal relation to gold by the abrogation of the gold clause in public and private debts; the domestic economy was separated from a rigid relation to the world economy by the abandonment of the gold standard and the rejection of the stabilization proposals of the London Economic Conference. These measures in the first hundred days of the New Deal placed the government in a position to determine monetary policy, a position which was strengthened when the Banking Act of 1935 transferred power over open market policies from New York to Washington. How well monetary policy has been conducted since this shift is a separate matter and one which I will come to later. What is immediately important is that this basic reform of our monetary system made monetary management a practical instrument of government.

A second major reform in the first hundred days was that of the credit structure. As a result of the long economic decline, the mortgage and credit markets were frozen and ineffective. The new administration provided for farm credit through the refinancing of farm mortgages and the creation of the Farm Credit organization. It unfroze the home mortgage market under the Home Owners Loan Act. It expanded the role of Hoover's Reconstruction Finance Corporation in making loans to business. All of these combined to make credit more available, and established principles of credit supply which have been followed subsequently to insure the widespread availability of credit beyond that which can be supplied through the banking system and the usual credit markets.

A third reform, and the most widely recognized, was in the field of social security. The principle of Federal responsibility at least under emergency conditions was adopted in setting up a national relief system and in establishing the Civilian Conservation Corps. Also, and more important, the creation of a permanent social security system was placed on the agenda at that time. The exact form and content was not yet clear. Study and discussion went on for a year and a half and finally crystallized in the Social Security Act of 1935. The reform in principle was an initial part of the New Deal, though its instrumentation took time.

A fourth reform came with respect to agriculture. The principle was accepted that farmers operating in a free market were vulnerable in an economy of big business and administered prices and that this situation required government intervention. That intervention first took the form of the Agricultural Adjustment Administration. When the Supreme Court found this form unacceptable, a modification was made in the form of intervention but not in the fact or the general purpose of intervention.

A fifth lasting reform was the use of fiscal policy to stimulate demand and employment. Hoover had operated with deficits against his will. But under the New Deal, deficits in a depression became a positive instrument of policy. This did not happen all at once. In the first hundred days, measures to balance the budget and measures to unbalance the budget for pump priming purposes were both passed. One group of advisors led by Lewis Douglas sponsored the Economy Act which cut government salaries and in other ways sought to reduce government expenditures. Other groups sponsored spending measures primarily for relief and public works, partly for their direct value and partly to act as pump primers, usually in the hope and expectation that when full employment was re-established the budget could be balanced. The net result was a substantial deficit in the first fiscal year of the New Deal and the resignation of Douglas. Thereafter deficits continued in spite of pressures to balance, while the principle of using fiscal policy as an instrument for stimulating demand gained ground with the spreading of the Keynesian thesis.

In these five cases of reform, four adopted in principle

and practice in the first hundred days and one advanced in theory and in effect acted on but subject to controversy, the aim was reasonably clear and the departure from orthodoxy was equally clear.

A sixth case, the National Recovery Administration and its industrial codes, is more complex. It contained some elements of permanent reform and some elements of a false direction. It is usually classed as one of the New Deal's failures. And yet I would class it as an outstanding success. Let me develop my reasons for this belief.

The NRA was never a single idea even though it often went under the head of industrial self-government. The drafting and passage of the act setting up NRA resulted in the main from the coalescence of four quite different groups with quite different objectives.

First, a large number of businessmen wanted to set aside the anti-trust laws so that the members of an industry could get together and prevent what was known as destructive price cutting or price chiseling. In the lexicon of classical theory, these terms have no meaning since prices are supposed to be made in the market and to adjust to equate supply and demand. But when industry operates through administered prices and administered wage rates, quite a different situation exists. The conditions which make price administration both possible and appropriate also provide the conditions in which price wars can be destructive, not only to the members of an industry but also to the public interest. On this point I will call your attention to the price wars between the railroads before rates were regulated. On one occasion a rate war brought the fare from New York to Chicago down to a single dollar. I cannot believe this was in the real interest of either the railroads or the public.

For the same reason, the industrial price wars set off by the Great Depression were in considerable degree destructive. They engendered wage cutting, thereby shrinking buying power as much as prices were lowered, and because of rigidities in the system, the lower prices created bankruptcy rather than recovery. The prime drive of business was to stop such price wars and selling below cost.

A second group that joined in creating the NRA was labor. The American Federation of Labor put on a drive to spread the work by shortening the work week to thirty hours and a bill to that effect was introduced into Congress. But the drive was diverted into the more flexible NRA which took account of this and other aims of labor.

A third group was composed of what might be called the industrial self-governors. This group included many leading businessmen such as W. Averell Harriman of the Chamber of Commerce and Gerard Swope of General Electric. It also included Hugh Johnson and Donald Richberg. The members of this group were public-spirited citizens and were concerned with more than the destructive price wars. They sought more comprehensive industrial self-government to improve the working of industry.

Finally there were those selective planners such as Rexford Tugwell who wanted to see a few specific and chaotic industries like bituminous coal brought into more rational organization.

The NRA bill that was finally passed reflected the combined impact of these four groups and received their support. Under the codes, all of the aims of these four groups were served in some degree. Through the codes, business was able to eliminate destructive price cutting and other disorganizing practices; in exchange for this abrogation of the anti-trust laws it agreed to regularize working conditions, raise substandard wage rates and accept collective bargaining. Industrial self-government was given a trial and some rationalization of particular industries was instituted or under study.

I will not go into the actual operation of NRA or its

demise, but I will point out three major values which I find in the NRA.

The first has to do with the temporary situation. You must remember that at that time, business was in a state of shock. Failure on every hand, cutthroat price wars, frozen credit, a collapsed banking system and a general feeling that the whole free enterprise system was going to pieces. At this point, action was more important than the right action. To the orthodox economist, the Blue Eagle parades look odd and the industrial codes look still odder if not subversive. But to the economic psychologist it is clear that they served a major function in setting business back on its feet and giving it a sense of direction. Price wars were halted and administered prices again bore a more reasonable relation to costs. The businessman could stop spending all his time worrying about whether he could stay in business and spend some of it on planning and producing.

This therapeutic value of NRA was a temporary matter. Once economic recovery was well launched, this function was completed. Business was no longer in shock and price wars were no longer a major cause of disruption. When the NRA was found unconstitutional just a month before its two years of legislative life were due to end, there was no pause in the rapid business recovery which continued for another two years.

The second great value I find in the NRA is that it established the principle of countervailing power on the part of labor. It established the principle that union organization and collective bargaining are in the public interest. Without the NRA and its Section 7a, I doubt if the Wagner Labor Act could have been passed. In the NRA, business was persuaded to accept collective bargaining by its desire for freedom from the anti-trust laws, and it became more used to collective bargaining in the development of industrial codes. When the NRA came to an end, the principle of collective bargaining was firmly established and in some degree accepted by business. The way had been prepared for the continuation of this basic reform through the Wagner Labor Act.

The third great value I find in the NRA is that it got the idea of industrial self-government out of our system. How far the concept of industrial self-government derived from fascist experience and how much it was indigenous is hard to tell. But for years, the inefficiencies and wastes arising from competition among the few had been apparent to observant and public-spirited businessmen. The search for improvement led many to the idea of industry-wide agreements aimed not at the making of monopoly profits but aimed at reducing waste and inefficiency. And, of course, others joined in who were primarily interested in profits. As long as depression continued, and probably after production and employment were restored, the pressure for industrial self-government would have continued.

The actual experience with industrial self-government under the industrial codes of NRA made the dangers of such self-government clear. Two things happened. Those who were primarily concerned with the public interest saw the process of self-government being used against the public interest and sought means to control these powers more nearly in the public interest. And while some progress was made in this direction, the task appeared herculean. Business on the other hand was beginning to see that industrial self-government would mean much more government intervention than had initially been envisaged. Thus, after two years of experience, the whole idea of industrial self-government was losing caste. Many who were for it initially were turning away. If the Supreme Court had not intervened, there is a real question whether NRA would have survived more than its legislative two years. It might be that it would have been continued for another year or two.

But as things were going, it seems to me most unlikely that it would have been continued much longer than this.

Thus, in my view the NRA served the three great purposes of overcoming business shock, acting as midwife to the permanent reform in labor-business relations, and discrediting the principle of industrial self-government. In retrospect, I think it came to an end at an appropriate time even though it left no solution to the wastes and inefficiencies involved in competition among the few.

Here I have covered the major reforms of the New Deal which derive from the Roosevelt Revolution and which have to do with the operating of the system as a whole. The establishment of monetary management; the creation of a more flexible system of credit; the establishment of social security; the support of agricultural income; the establishment of collective bargaining and the use of a government deficit to create buying power. All of these except the use of deficits I find established as policy in the first hundred days of the New Deal. And even the pump priming role of deficit spending was beginning to be recognized. There are other elements of New Deal action, such as the regulation of the security exchanges, the break-up of holding companies, and the reciprocal trade agreements, which were important to economic development, but these were just as consistent with orthodox thinking, once the abuses were recognized, as they were to the post-revolution viewpoint. Likewise there were specific activities of the New Deal which grew directly out of the new point of view, such as the TVA and the Rural Electrification Act but were not directly concerned with the over-all problem of making a modern free enterprise system work.

The initial effect of the New Deal measures was to create four years of steady and rapid recovery. In four years industrial production doubled and was back to its 1929 peak. Real income had increased more than 50 percent and was likewise back to the peak of 1929. This striking recovery, however, did not give full production and employment. The labor force had increased since 1929 and productivity had also increased. But another year and a half of continued rise would have established full employment. All of this was a remarkable achievement.

However, it must not be thought that these reforms provided a coherent theory of operation. They still represented pieces of theory that seemed to be working. There was no comprehensive and coherent theory accepted as a guide to policy. There was not yet a new tangent to the changed reality. Instead there was much controversy over why the programs were working. In this controversy Keynes' theory of employment played an important part.

This controversy was raised to a high pitch by the recession of 1937-38. I don't think there is even yet general agreement as to just why the down-turn came. In my own view it was primarily the result of two developments, which I will discuss because they throw light on the lack of coherence in New Deal thinking.

First the budget was inadvertently brought into balance. I say "inadvertently" because it was not a planned balance. It was expected that a budget deficit would be reduced but that there would still be a significant deficit with its pump priming effect. And, if you look at the orthodox budget, this expectation was realized. But a new factor had entered in—the tax revenue from the newly instituted Social Security program. In Treasury accounting this revenue was recorded as a receipt and then charged as a budget expense when the receipts were placed in the Social Security reserve. The deficit of the orthodox budget covered up the fact that on a cash basis, that is on the basis of money taken from the public and paid back to the public, the national budget was balanced. Fiscal policy no longer provided a net stimulus to buying power.

The second factor contributing to the recession, and I

believe the more important one, had to do with monetary management. In the first four years of the New Deal monetary management powers had been used to bring about a steady increase in the money supply so that by the beginning of 1937 there was 60 percent more money in circulation than in 1933. Then money measures were taken which brought the monetary expansion to an end and instituted a moderate contraction. This meant that neither fiscal nor monetary policy was contributing to further recovery. Indeed recovery did not resume until the middle of 1938 when monetary expansion was resumed and a mild deficit renewed.

This halt in recovery was, I believe, largely a product of confusion and disagreement on policy. Fiscal and monetary policy had not yet come into its own as the prime instrument for maintaining full employment. Nor was the role of monetary policy clear.

The actual situation was one worthy of Greek drama. At the Treasury we had Henry Morgenthau, a strong adherent of a balanced budget who would accept an unbalanced budget in loyalty to Roosevelt but was constantly pressing for balance and was supported by Daniel W. Bell, the Director of the Budget. At the Federal Reserve Board we had Marriner Eccles who was a strong believer in fiscal policy as an instrument of recovery but relied extensively on Loughlin Currie, his economic advisor, who was an ardent Keynesian; Currie believed with Keynes that once interest rates were brought down by monetary expansion, further monetary expansion would have no significant effect in expanding demand and employment.

Thus we had something in the nature of a stalemate, with the Treasury not pushing deficit spending as a recovery measure and the Federal Reserve Board not pushing monetary action. It was primarily the demand arising from the approaching war, not New Deal policy, which completed the economic recovery. Indeed, full employment was only just about achieved by the time of Pearl Harbor. While the New Deal had created the instruments for achieving full employment it had not learned how to use them effectively. There was not yet a comprehensive theory tangent to the new reality.

In appraising this stalemate in theory and practice, I place particular responsibility on a flaw in Keynes' reasoning. He argued that the only way monetary expansion would affect demand for goods and thereby employment was through the lowering of interest rates, and when interest rates reached a minimum level further expansion in the money supply would cease to be stimulating. Others argued that the supply of money affected the level of demand both through the interest rate and directly through its impact on the propensities to consume and invest. If Keynes was correct, once interest rates were brought down, further monetary expansion would not help recovery. If the second view was correct, monetary expansion could be effective regardless of low interest rates.

World War II put a temporary end to this controversy, but at the end of the war it was given a remarkable test in the efforts of both sides to estimate postwar unemployment —a test which the physical scientists might refer to as the crucial experiment. From the beginning of 1942 when full employment was finally reached to the end of the war, the money supply had been nearly doubled while there had been no great increase in the price level. The controversy was then focused on whether the big increase in the money supply would modify demand. The followers of Keynes said, "No, since interest rates are already low, the increase in the money supply can be disregarded." The opposite view was that the large money supply would act as a stimulant to demand. On the basis of their theory the Keynesians forecast that demand would be too low to give full employment and that unemployment in the following June, after demobilization, would be in the neighborhood of 8 to 9 million. On the basis of the huge increase in the supply, I forecast unemployment the following June at somewhere around 2.5 million. There was nothing like 8 or 9 million unemployed in June of 1946. In fact, unemployment was very close to my figure.

This failure of the Keynesian forecast has, I believe, been increasingly recognized in confirming this flaw in Keynes' analysis. But what is important here is that after six years of the New Deal no coherent theory had been accepted for the role of government in the working of a free enterprise system in which the big corporation and administered price plays a major role. When war shifted the focus of government, the acceptable solution to this problem still lay ahead.

So far I have been giving my own interpretation of the Roosevelt Revolution out of my own experience in it. Those who have read Arthur Schlesinger Jr.'s able and brilliant history of *The Age of Roosevelt* will recognize that in the main the two accounts are consistent. But in one important respect they differ, that of the continuity of the New Deal.

Schlesinger divides the first four years of the Roosevelt administration into two equal periods which he designates the First New Deal and the Second New Deal, each of which, he says, involved a quite different orientation. He draws a dichotomy between the planning orientation in the first period and an orientation toward the break-up of bigness to make the classical market work in the second period. I believe there was such variety of thinking and such a pragmatic approach throughout the whole period that there is no basis for talking of a "first" and a "second" New Deal.

It is true that there was more talk of production planning in the first period and less talk in the second. But both production planning on the one hand and the re-creation of the classical model on the other were extreme views.

And the difference in the weight of discussion finds little reflection in the actual policies of the two periods. In the first two years, outside of agriculture, there were no measures of production planning and in the second, no measures to break up big manufacturing business.

If one looks at what was done in these four years and not at what was talked, the second half is a direct continuation or outgrowth of most of the major policies of the first. The main drive throughout gave less emphasis to economic planning than was suggested by those extremists who advocated production planning, and more emphasis on planning than was suggested by those extremists who sought a return to small enterprise and laissez-faire.

Most New Dealers sensed the fundamental changes in the structure of the market and tried to adapt public policy to them. In both periods the major measures were directed to adapting public policy to the changed structure. Policies adopted or implicit in the first two years were given permanent form in the following two years. The Bank Reform Act, the Social Security Act, the Wagner Act, heavy income and inheritance taxes, the planned use of fiscal policy to stimulate demand, in fact most of the major policies and legislation of the second period, were just as much in conflict with the principles of laissez-faire and the classical model as were those of the first period.

Thus, in my view the Roosevelt Revolution was a complete turning away from the classical model. Roosevelt's pragmatic and experimental approach to the new frontiers opened up by this revolution was a search for policies consistent both with the changed market structure and with a democratic society. In this search both the extremes of production planning and of laissez-faire were rejected, and a solid foundation was laid toward a middle way.

Since the New Deal, we have had two wars and some years of unstable peace. We have made much progress in solidifying the foundation the New Deal laid. The responsibility of government toward employment has been formalized in the Employment Act of 1946, and monetary and fiscal policy have been generally accepted as the major instruments for maintaining demand. Social Security has been extended and is likely to be further extended. And in other ways there has been progress in carrying out the implications of the Roosevelt Revolution. We are well on our way.

But we are not there yet. There still remain important parts of the frontiers opened up by the Roosevelt Revolution which remain undeveloped.

First, there is the problem of maintaining full production and employment. The acceptance of monetary and fiscal measures toward this end does not determine the relative role of each or just how the job should be done. Recurring recessions and economic restriction make this point, as do the difficulties of controlling administrative inflation and of adjusting our international balance of payments. Until this issue is determined the streamlining of the institutions for fiscal and monetary management cannot be effectively carried out.

Second, the pricing powers of big business and big labor and the wastes and inefficiencies arising out of competition among the few still remain far from a satisfactory solution.

Third, the principles to guide the use of natural resources remain indeterminate.

Fourth, our Social Security system is far from complete.

And finally, the appropriate role of planning in a democratic free enterprise system still remains a challenge.

Not until these problems are accepted, solved and built into a coherent system of policy for the big-business, administered-price economy will we have the necessary guide for making a modern free enterprise system work effectively. Only then will our theory again be tangent to the curve of reality.

CHAPTER THREE

Collective Capitalism and Economic Theory

The following essay was first given in 1957 as a Marshall Wythe Lecture at the College of William and Mary at Williamsburg, Virginia. It was subsequently published in Science *and, with minor modification, in the* Harvard Business Review. *It is concerned more directly with the implications of the corporate revolution for economic theory.*

THE MODERN CORPORATION has undermined the preconceptions of classical economic theory as effectively as the quantum undermined classical physics at the beginning of the twentieth century. An equally drastic reconstruction of economic theory is due and is, perhaps, now in process. It is my purpose here to present a background for this reconstruction. This I propose to do by examining the relation between recent events and economic theory.

But first let us consider the role of theory in human action. In a basic sense man is a systematic animal. We live by systems of thought which guide our actions. Whether the particular system of thought is that of the witch doctor or the modern scientist, a system built around concepts of freedom and democracy or around a single God and the Ten Commandments, we could not live our lives effectively without such systems of thought. The real world is altogether too complex to be grasped. We build simplified systems of thought in order to aid our action. And these simplified systems are our theories about the real world.

Now it is a fundamental characteristic of our systems of

thought that they never fit reality exactly. We can expect at best only a rough fit. A theory may be highly complex and logically consistent, and yet it is beyond wisdom to make it take account of *all* the real facts. As an approximation, a theory may serve us well. Newton's theory of gravity is sufficiently accurate for everyday purposes. But we should recognize that a theory can never be so complete as to give a perfect fit to reality.

In the field of the social sciences the crudeness in the fit of theory to reality is of particular importance because the social reality can itself be changing relative to the theory. It is for this reason that I think of society as moving in a curve of change and a social theory as a straight line which may or may not be tangent to the curve at a particular time. When the theory is tangent to the curve, at that time the theory fits the reality well enough so that good policy can be made in terms of the theory, even though the theory does not exactly fit the facts.

But then the social reality may change. The tangent of theory and the curve of reality get farther and farther apart. Policies made in terms of the theory fail to produce good results.

I believe that we are now in a period in which society has moved out from under our older economic theories and that a new or revised set of theories is now in process of development. It is my purpose here to show why new theories are needed to guide policy, and also to suggest some of the directions the new theories seem likely to take.

The "straight-line" character of social theory arises from the basic assumptions of any given theory. A given theory can be elaborated within the framework of its own logic, but it is confined to the limits of its own assumptions. More cannot be derived from a theory than is put in by assumption. Let us see how this works in the case of economic theory.

Types of Control over Production

For economic theorizing, we can distinguish between at least four basic types of nongovernmental production which differ as to who controls production and can imagine economic models, each made up of just one type of production.

We might assume a subsistence model in which each economic unit produces only for its own consumption and in which there is no buying and selling. In approximation, such a model describes the economic condition of the Virginia settlements before tobacco exports became a significant factor, it describes most of our early pioneer settlements as our population moved west, and it still applies to some mountain homesteads. But, more importantly, this model applies in considerable degree to more than half of the present-day population of the world—to the Indian village, to the African tribesmen, and to people in many other parts of the world. For such people the market plays a negligible role, and production is organized within the village or tribe on a collective basis to meet the needs of the producers who are also the consumers. In such subsistence economies, consumers are in control of production or, what is more significant for our present analysis, consumer, worker, owner, and management are combined in a single economic unit. As a result, production policy and the instruments of production are controlled by units which combine the interests of consumer, worker, owner, and management.

Or we might assume an economic model in which individuals produce goods for sale in the market and buy goods in the market for consumption but in which no one works directly for anyone else. In such an economy, price and the market serve to organize the production of separate economic units. This form of production is typified by most American farms—a single producer raising cash crops, selling the product into the market, and taking out of the market what he needs for production and for consumption. If all production were carried on by such one-man enterprises, we would have a pure atomistic economy, with the consumer no longer in direct control of production but influencing production only through the market. In such an economy, direct control over production policy and the instruments of production would rest with individuals who combine the interests of worker-owner-manager, while the interests of consumers would depend on market forces. It is the great achievement of Adam Smith that he presented a theory of market behavior for such an atomistic economy. I will come back to this in a moment.

A third type of economy which we might assume is one in which production is carried on under the factory system with individual factory owners managing production but hiring workers to do the main producing. In such an economy, not only the consumer but also the worker is separated from control over production policy and the instruments of production, except as consumer and worker affect production through the market. This system of production has properly been called private capitalism, and it was factory production which provided the basic assumption of Marxian theory, while the separation of the worker from control over the instruments of production provided the basis of his class struggle.

A fourth type of economic model which we might assume is one in which all production is carried on by great corporate units in which ownership is so widely dispersed that owners, as well as consumers and workers, are separated from control over production policy and the instruments of production. In such an economy, management would be in control, subject, of course, to the influence of the markets for goods, for labor, and for securities. And with the separation of ownership and control comes the possibility of great aggregations of productive activity. We now have single corporate enterprises employing hundreds of thousands of workers, having hundreds of thousands of stockholders, using billions of dollars' worth of the instruments of production, serving millions of customers, and controlled by a single management group. These are great collectives of enterprise, and a system composed of them, or dominated by them might well be called "collective capitalism."

It would be possible to elaborate other types of economy such as the Soviet Government ownership and control, or an economy of cooperatives, but those outlined here will serve the present purpose.

Actually, the history of Europe and America in the last four centuries roughly fits the pattern of these four economies, though at no period was the economy exclusively of one type or another. The feudal economy of Europe and the pioneer economies of America were primarily of the subsistence type; Adam Smith's eighteenth-century economy was dominantly atomistic; the nineteenth-century economy was dominated by the factory system; and today the big corporation gives its particular character to our modern economy. Let us then trace economic theory in relation to the curve of our changing economy.

Economic Theory and the Real Economy

We can begin with classical economic theory, which for present purposes starts with Adam Smith and comes down through Mill and Marshall. This body of theory, *in its essentials*, relates to an atomistic economy and never really grapples with the problems which make a factory economy different from an atomistic economy. This assertion may surprise some since, certainly, the determination of wage rates was one of the classical problems. But consider that in classical theory, labor was treated as a commodity. In an atomistic economy, the shoemaker bought leather and shoe pegs and twine, combined them into a pair of shoes, and sold the shoes. And in classical theory the shoe manufacturer bought leather and shoe pegs and twine *and labor*, combined them into a pair of shoes, and sold the shoes. The factory system brought no change in theory except the delineation of a special commodity, labor, for which there were especially interesting problems of demand and supply. At the same time, the worker himself was treated as an entrepreneur seeking to market his "product"—labor.

A single example will help to underline this fact. Ever since I became aware of the limited basis of classical theory, I have sought cases where a classical scholar has made a *significant* theoretical point which would apply to a factory economy and could not apply to an atomistic economy. So far, prior to Keynes, I have found only a single case. It occurs in D. H. Robertson's brilliant little book, *Banking Policy and the Price Level*. Robertson points out that if price and production policy in a company or an industry were made by the owners, one policy would result, whereas if policy were made jointly by owners and workers, a different policy would result, with lower prices and larger volume, since instead of seeking to maximize profits, the joint policy would seek to maximize the sum of profits and wages. Such a statement would make no sense in a pre-factory system in which there was no separation of the worker from control over production policy.

Although there may be other examples of such a departure from the assumption of an atomistic economy, I believe they are few and far between and have not produced modifications in classical theory. They do not stand in the way of the conclusion that, for practical purposes, classical theory is built on the basic assumption of an atomistic economy; we apply the classical analysis and classical conclusions to a factory or corporate economy at our peril.

Karl Marx took a big step forward in building his economic theory on the assumption of a factory economy and private capitalism. He recognized the separation of worker from control over the instruments of production and rejected the idea of treating labor as a commodity. In this he was more realistic than the classical theorists. On the other hand, he built a body of theory which has clearly been proved wrong in this country and certainly has not been supported so far by events in the Soviet Union. In this country, instead of progressive exploitation, there has been remarkable improvement in the workers' lot—the poor have become richer—while in the Soviet Union the workers are being exploited for the purposes of the state, with a real question whether the people are better off as a result. For Marx' theory, the superiority of his basic assumption of a factory economy does not make up for the weakness in his theoretical analysis.

As for collective capitalism, no comprehensive economic theory has been developed in terms of such an economy, in spite of the fact that the collective enterprise of our great corporations sets the tone of today's economy. As a result, we stand with a great deal of economic theory, but a major part of it was built on an obsolete base, and another part has been disproved by events. It is clear to me that a major reconstruction of economic theory is in order. We must create a body of theory which applies to collective capitalism and modify it to the extent necessary to allow for the fact that not all enterprise is collective enterprise.

Steps toward the Reconstruction of Economic Theory

The first step in a reconstruction of economic theory is to define its scope in modern terms. As long as economics dealt only with a pure atomistic economy (or with the theoretical equivalent, a factory economy with labor treated as a commodity), the scope of economic theory could be limited to the market mechanism and to a consideration of the ways in which individual behavior affected and in turn was affected by the market. For such an economy, an analysis of the market is also an analysis of the way in which the activities of separate individuals are coordinated in using resources to satisfy human wants. Some economists would like to limit the scope of economic theory today to the operation of the market mechanism. But today, with the great role played by corporate management in coordinating the activity of separate individuals within an enterprise, it is obvious that the market mechanism is not the only coordinating device. If we limit economic theory to the market, we are leaving out a major part of economic co-ordination. I believe that economic theory must be given the broader scope and that it must deal with economic coordination within enterprises as well as between enterprises. It must be concerned with the coordination of individual action in using resources to satisfy human wants, however that coordination is brought about.

If we accept this broad scope for economic theory, the second step is to investigate the various means by which economic coordination is brought about. So far, I have been able to discover four distinct and important ways by which the economic actions of individuals can be coordinated. The first and most obvious is the market mechanism. I do not need to point out how the market can coordinate the productive activity of thousands of individuals. A second and equally obvious method of coordination is by administrative direction. The manager tells *A* to do one thing, *B* another, and *C* a third, and, because the manager planned it that way, the separate actions of the three fall into a common pattern. But there are two other devices of coordination which are not so obvious, and yet they are particularly important for a democratic society. These devices are what might be called canalizing rules and the acceptance of common goals.

We are all familiar with the canalizing rules—the laws, rules, and customs—which help to coordinate daily living. The rule that one drives on the right side of the road or the custom that bills are sent out at the end of the month helps to bring order into individual behavior. Or consider two people getting into an elevator. It is much easier for a man and a woman to enter than it is for two polite men to do so. These are perhaps trivial examples. More important are the custom of accepting money in exchange for goods, the laws enforcing contracts, and the rules and regulations set up by a corporation to facilitate its activity. The canalizing rules play a major role in coordinating the activities of separate individuals.

The fourth coordinating influence is the acceptance of common goals. We had an outstanding example of this during World War II. There was a nation-wide acceptance of the aim of winning the war. And, in the light of this common goal, any number of people did things or put up with things in ways to contribute to the war effort without being told. Or take a more homely example. A family decides to go on a picnic and, without specific instructions, various members in the family start to prepare. Some make sandwiches, some get the car ready, and others get out the picnic hamper. Once the picnic goal has been accepted, coordination can come simply as a result of the thinking and action of each individual as he sees how his effort can be coordinated with that of others. Business enterprise is constantly using goals both to stimulate and to coordinate production and sales. We will come back later to the coordinating role of common goals.

For our present analysis, what is important is that there are at least four ways in which the action of individuals can be coordinated to a greater or lesser degree, and, in any concrete situation, coordination may involve two or more of these different methods. I believe that economic theory must take account of all four.

With this background, let us consider the various areas of economic theory and the direction in which they are developing or should develop because of the facts of collective capitalism. For this purpose I will distinguish between the following four major areas of economic theory: the theory of employment; the theory of the firm; the theory of allocation; and the theory of economic planning.

Employment Theory

The term *employment theory* is relatively new, but classical theory dealt with the problem of under-utilization of resources under the heading of Say's law and in the equilibrium equations of Walras. According to both, the only condition of equilibrium in an atomistic economy is one of full use of resources. As Mill pointed out, according to classical theory general overproduction was impossible—except, of course, temporary overproduction, which would quickly correct itself.

Actual events—the long American depression of the 1890's, Britain's long depression in the 1920's, the world-wide depression of the 1930's, and the long history of business fluctuations—finally broke the hold of Say's law and the belief in a self-correcting mechanism that would maintain reasonably full employment. Keynes came forward with a new theory of employment which he believed would explain the possibility of equilibrium at less than full employment in a competitive and flexible-price economy.

For many years this theory found wide acceptance and helped to make theoretically respectable the rejection of Say's law. But in spite of the brilliance of Keynes' analysis, it rested on an assumption that is no longer generally accepted by economists—the assumption that the only way a change in the real stock of money could affect the level of demand and employment is through changes in the level of interest rates. I cannot go into detail here. It is sufficient to say that the statistical evidence does not support Keynes' assumption. Keynes has not supplied an explanation of unemployment for an economy of flexible prices and wage rates. For such an atomistic economy, the only condition of equilibrium would appear to be one of full employment;

Say's law would still seem to hold for an atomistic economy.

But our present-day economy is not an economy of flexible prices and wage rates. The factory system and the modern corporation have brought changes which must be taken into the basic assumptions of theory. Labor is not a commodity, and wage rates are not flexible but a form of administered prices. In addition, administration of enterprise has extended into the goods market, and we also have administered prices for goods. When economic theory is rebuilt on the basis of administered prices and administered wage rates, I believe the inapplicability of Say's law and the Walrasian full-employment equilibrium will be obvious.

First let us consider wage rates. Classical theory had no difficulty picturing a commodity market for wheat or oranges with suppliers and demanders brought into adjustment by price. But have you ever run across a theoretical description of a market for labor in which the wage rate equates the demand and supply of labor? I never have, and I have never been able to envisage such a market. Would each worker come into the market each day and offer a basket full of "labor," and would employers "buy" a fresh lot of labor each day? This just does not make sense. A worker cannot sell his labor apart from himself; an enterprise cannot use labor apart from the persons who constitute it. And an essential part of the value of "labor" to an enterprise is the familiarity of the persons constituting "labor" with the equipment or affairs of the enterprise employing them. This means that a free market and flexible prices for labor are not feasible if big factory or corporate enterprise is to be efficient.

In actual fact, as I have said, wage rates are a form of "administered price." Before labor became organized, the typical procedure for establishing wage rates was administrative. In starting up a factory, the manager decided on what wage rates he would pay for each type of work and sent out word that jobs were available. If the supply of job seekers at those wage rates was larger than the number he wanted to hire, he would turn some away. If the supply was not as large as he wanted, he would send word farther afield, or perhaps he would send out recruiting agents to bring in workers. Thus the wage rates set by the manager would equate supply and demand only by chance. In most cases, either demand or supply would be in excess. And, what is most important for employment theory, the fact of a discrepancy between the supply and demand for labor would not lead the manager to alter his wage rates unless the discrepancy was considerable. Similarly, once a factory was in operation, if the manager needed fewer workers, he would lay off a part of his labor force. But he was unlikely to reduce his schedule of wage rates unless there was a very large increase in unemployment or unless his own firm was being seriously squeezed by competition. Thus, under the factory system, and even without labor organization, wage rates were administered and tended to be relatively inflexible, seldom closely equating the supply and demand for labor.

Whether or not the organization of labor has increased the inflexibility of wage rates is not clear. During the Great Depression of the early 1930's, wage rates dropped more in the clothing trades in which labor organization was strong than they did in such durable-goods industries as automobiles and electric equipment where unemployment was greater, labor was weak, and wage rates were administered by the corporate management. On the other hand, negotiated wage contracts certainly limit the power of management to change wage rates for periods of time. For present purposes it is immaterial whether the organization of labor increases the inflexibility of wage rates or simply confirms a behavior which management would have adopted in any case. What is important is that the factory system and the corporate system involve wage rates which do not behave like the classical commodity prices.

Administration of prices has also come to be a dominant characteristic of our factory and corporate economy. A company will set its price for a product and hold it constant for a period of time, selling whatever amount is demanded at the administered price. Demand at the administered price may be in excess of supply, as was recently the case with steel. Or demand may be less than the company is willing to supply at the administered price. As a result, an administered price will equate supply and demand only by chance, while an excess of supply or demand of considerable magnitude may develop without resulting in a revision of an administered price.

The classical theorists were familiar with administered prices, but, so far as I know, administered prices were never introduced as a basic assumption in classical economic theory. Their effect was treated as a matter of "friction" which slowed up but did not prevent the process of automatic adjustment. But today a large proportion of all labor and commodity transactions in this country take place at administered prices. Certainly most retail distribution, including a large part of food distribution, is at administered prices. So are most manufactured products and most of the services. Only in farm products and raw materials is the classical market price the general rule, and even here there are many exceptions. Thus, the factory and corporate systems provide us with administered prices, as well as administered wage rates, both of which lie outside of classical theory.

Once one introduces administered prices and wage rates as basic assumptions in employment theory, it is not difficult to explain equilibrium at less than full employment. Keynes did this, not as a theory, but as a device of exposition. When he analyzed the effect on employment of changes in the propensities to consume and invest, he first assumed that prices and wage rates were fixed. This was only a device to make it easier to follow his analysis, and he has made it clear that his conclusions on employment did not depend on this temporary assumption. Yet perhaps his greatest claim to fame will be this inadvertent introduction of a formulation of equilibrium with fixed prices and wage rates.

Of course, administered prices and wage rates are subject to change, and the new theory of employment must take account of the successive re-adjustment of prices and wage rates as the discrepancy between supply and demand exceeds some threshold of administrative action. The theory must be concerned both with the magnitude of this discrepancy and with the magnitude of the price revision when it is made. What is immediately important is that, when administered prices and wage rates are assumed, it is easy to construct economic models which reach short-run equilibrium at less than full employment and in which automatic forces operate toward full employment so slowly that they are not important. Thus, in one plausible model which I constructed, the automatic forces would restore full employment only after an infinite regression in time.

Here, then, is a major reconstruction of economic theory required by the actual characteristics of our economy. Fortunately, our practice in seeking to maintain full employment has run ahead of dependable theory. But a dependable theory of employment could greatly clarify the essential role of government and greatly increase the efficiency of practice in this field.

The problem here is to develop a statement of short-run economic equilibrium on the assumptions that some prices are of the classical type and that some are administered. We have the Walrasian formulation of equilibrium for an economy of perfectly flexible prices. We have the Keynesian formulation with its ambiguity about price, but it is capable of stating an equilibrium with prices fixed. What we need is a Walrasian-like formulation which will state the condition of equilibrium if some prices are administered and some prices are flexible, and indicate how changes in the equilibrium-determining factors will alter the equilibrium result.

Theory of the Firm

A second area of economic theory which needs reconstruction because of the modern corporation is the theory of the firm. This presents a many-issued problem, one that is at the heart of economic theory, since assumptions about the behavior of the firm enter into all other areas of economic theory.

Classical economics has given us a highly elaborated theory of the behavior of a firm—and here I include not only the classical line through Marshall but also the somewhat arid analyses of Chamberlin and Robinson. This theory is concerned with the firm as a buyer, combiner or producer, and seller of goods. And because labor is treated as a commodity, it applies primarily to an atomistic economy. The theory itself starts with the assumption that the entrepreneur is seeking to maximize his profit and works out the different patterns of behavior which would maximize profit under various known conditions.

This theory, when it is applied to imperfect competition, has always given me a good deal of trouble, even as applied to an atomistic economy. But let us assume that the classical theory of the firm does apply to the small entrepreneur in an atomistic economy or is so modified that it does apply, and ask what modifications are needed to make it fit the corporate firms of collective capitalism.

The first change is implicit in our discussion of employment theory: the new theory of the enterprise must account for the well-nigh universal presence of administered prices and wage rates and their respective behavior. There is nothing in the classical theory of the profit-maximizing firm which would lead one to expect administered prices or administered wage rates.

A second change was pointed out by Adolf Berle and me in our book, *The Modern Corporation and Private Property*, in which we indicated how the separation of ownership and control in most of our big corporations undercuts the function of profits to owners as a stimulus to more efficient operation of the enterprise. Consider first the profits going to those stockholders who do not in fact control the enterprise or make policy. Such profits cannot act as an incentive to better operation of the enterprise. And if, instead, profits over and above the amount necessary to induce investment were to go to the controlling management so they would induce more efficient operations, as profit theory would require, the courts would find this illegal, because the profits "belong" to the stockholders.

On the other hand, how much do profits from ownership act as a stimulus to those in control of a big corporation whose stock is widely dispersed? It is often said that, even though a controlling group may own only a small proportion of a company's stock, their ownership interest and the incentives arising from it can still be large because of the size of the company. Let us look at this for a minute. Consider, for example, a memorandum recently circulated by the Atchison, Topeka, and Santa Fe Railway Company giving the stockholdings of the directors of the company who are, in effect, in control of that corporation. In combination, the directors hold one-tenth of 1 percent of the outstanding stock. The average stockholding per director has a current market value of approximately $50,000, and the largest holding by a director is just under $200,000. These are sizable amounts of investment. But do they really supply a significant inducement to strive vigorously to increase the company's profit? Suppose that, by more vigorous direction, the company could be made to yield 20 percent higher profits. Assuming that this would mean a 20 percent higher dividend, the average director would get $600 more in dividends, while the director with the largest stockholding would get four times this amount. And since most of the directors, if not all, are already paying income taxes at the more robust rates, only a part of the $600 would be a reward. My own belief is that the directors of such a well-run railroad as the Santa Fe try to run it well for the same reasons that the trustees of a great university seek to run the university well. In the case of the Santa Fe, profits are a symbol of successful operations, but I question how far the receipt of profits by the controlling directors *through their ownership* is a dominant stimulus to efficient operation.

I am not here suggesting that profits do not play an important role in big corporate enterprise. I am suggesting that their role may be quite different from that attributed to profits in the representative small firm of classical theory. As a minimum, we can say that profits cannot perform their traditional role where ownership and control are separated, for this traditional role depended on the assumption that ownership and control were combined. We should start fresh and ask just what are the motivations of top corporate management—to increase their personal incomes, to serve the stockholders, to expand management's power, to foster the status of the corporate collective, to serve the public interest? Clearly, a new theory of the firm to apply to the corporate collective must start with an analysis of motivation in the big business bureaucracies. Such an analysis must be based on actual observation. This will not be easy, because motivation is itself elusive. Perhaps such investigations will require the joint action of economist, political scientist, psychologist and anthropologist. Until such studies are made, our basis for assuming motivation is inadequate.

In the meantime, I offer the suggestion that a study of motivation in the top management of a great university would throw more light on the motivation of top corporate management than any amount of study of small private enterprises. Like a university, the great corporate collective is a "going concern" with its own momentum and its own internal drives and internal conflicts. Literature is beginning to reflect this in such books and plays as *Executive Suite* and *The Solid Gold Cadillac*. How far is the task of top management in the corporation that of generating and sustaining group thinking and group decision-making? And what factors actually enter into top management decisions?

There are also problems of motivation in the lesser ranks of management. Are the pressures for conformity and compromise in the group activities of management reducing initiative and enterprise, either by suppressing it or by selecting away from it? Are the great corporations creating a new "economic man"—the "organization man"—with new characteristics which the economist will have to understand, analyze, and take into account? And can the "organization man" be adequate to fill the shoes of top management?

The bureaucratization of industry requires still another extension of the theory of the firm—the study of the bureaucracy itself. How are the great corporations actually run? How are the activities of 100,000 persons coordinated within a single enterprise? What kind of organization makes for effective use of resources; what kind, for wasteful use? With so much of the coordination of individual activity brought about through administrative action within single units, how does this affect the use of resources in the satisfying of wants? In some degree this aspect of enterprise theory must deal with the same problems of administration as those dealt with by political theory in its analysis of government bureaucracy, but in other respects, particularly in its focus on the impact of administration on the use of resources, this will be a new kind of allocation theory in which the unseen hand of Adam Smith is replaced by the visible hand of business bureaucracy.

The reconstituted theory of the firm will also have to take account of corporate politics as well as corporate economics. The modern corporation is more than a legal framework of enterprise. It is an institution for interrelating the interests of security holders, workers, consumers, and management. As such, it is a focus for conflicting, as well as common, interests, and it is the focus of power conflicts. Just where in these power conflicts economics leaves off and political science begins is not at all clear. Perhaps what we need is a new joint science which gives new content to the old term *political economy* and applies it to the politico-economic formation of policy in the great corporate enterprises as well as in government.

Finally, the theory of the corporate firm will have to consider the public responsibility of corporate management arising from size and from the separation of control from consumer, worker, and owner alike. In our book on the modern corporation, Berle and I suggested that, if the controlling management of the big dispersely owned corporations adopted the role of arbiter between stockholders, workers, and consumers, the courts might accept such a role. Certainly there is considerable evidence that the larger corporations are accepting some degree of social responsibility as a step toward their own long-run status and survival. The theory of the collective firm must therefore consider under what conditions, if any, an enterprise can operate to serve the public interest without itself assuming any social responsibility; and also under what conditions an enterprise is so large or so relates investors, workers, and consumers that it must take into account, or be made to take into account, considerations of social interest as well as those of corporate profits.

When we have an adequate theory of the collective corporate firm, we will be able to picture an economic model of big corporate enterprise. Such a theory, combined with adequate theories of the firm for an atomistic and for a factory economy, should give us the basis for understanding most firm behavior in our actual complex economy.

Allocation Theory

The third great branch of economics I propose to discuss is allocation theory. Classical allocation theory rests on or includes the traditional theory of the firm and is concerned with the process by which scarce resources are allocated to different uses. It starts with the assumption of full employment and deals with the way in which prices and the market mechanism operate to direct resources into the production and distribution of the goods most in demand. Marshall's *Principles* represents the greatest formulation of this theory. It has been much elaborated since Marshall's time, but a great deal of the elaboration is to be found, at least in embryo, in Marshall's footnotes.

Certain basic assumptions of this theory are clear. Besides the assumption of full employment, the theory postulates Marshall's representative firm with ownership and control combined in a single owner or partnership. It treats labor as a commodity. And it assumes flexible prices which adjust to equate supply and demand. With these postulates, Marshall purports to show that, in general, prices (including wage rates) will so adjust that price and marginal cost will tend to be approximately equal, resources will tend to be used in the most productive manner, and the rewards to the factors of production will tend to be close to their respective marginal contributions to production. This theory is of great importance today because a great deal of private and public policy is built upon it, either consciously or unconsciously.

Now I do not wish to raise here the question of whether the conclusions of this theory logically flow from its postulates. The significant question is whether these same conclusions would flow if we postulated, not Marshall's representative firm, but the modern corporation with its vast size and the separation of ownership and control; if we postulated, not labor as a commodity, but labor as a group of human beings; if we postulated, not flexible prices which equate supply and demand, but administered prices under which supply and demand can be different. As far as I know, there is no one who has developed a coherent theory which rests on such modern postulates and develops their implications.

I have not done much work in the field of allocation theory, having been primarily concerned with employment theory, but I can at least lay down some questions which should challenge attention.

Let us consider an economic model in which all economic production is carried on by four hundred huge corporations. Let us also say that, at the outset, while each company produces many products, there are only four companies producing each particular commodity and that each has its own particular brands with their own characteristics; that labor, unlike a commodity, has created labor unions, and that wage rates are made by collective bargaining between unions and individual companies; and that the individual companies offer and promote the sales of their products at administered prices which are seldom changed except as quite large changes in costs or demand occur; and finally, that we start with full employment. How would such an economy run?

You will notice that I have excluded price wars by assumption. With only four producers of a commodity and with a considerable degree of product differentiation, competition can express itself in greater advertising expenditures, increased product differentiation, product improvement, and other means which seek to take business away from competitors or to expand the market. But the knowledge that a price cut will be met or surpassed by a competitor will inhibit price cuts, except to adjust to a considerable change in cost or demand.

I would also raise the question whether even a major change in demand would affect price. At a recent meeting of businessmen and economists, the head of one of our big retail and manufacturing enterprises argued that demand had no influence on prices and challenged the economists present to show how an increase in the demand for the products of his company would lead to his charging higher prices. In his thinking, prices were determined by costs and probably, for his particular firm, he was essentially right. Of course, it was easy to suggest that many raw materials have flexible prices which are sensitive to changes in demand and that, when the demand for his products increased, he increased orders and thereby increased the demand for raw materials somewhere back along the line and that this ultimately raised his costs. But suppose that raw materials were produced only by a few companies and these companies also operated with inflexible, administered prices. Under what conditions would changes in demand have an effect on prices? How large a change in demand would be necessary to trigger a change in price? And what relation could be expected between marginal cost and price?

Then consider the question of profits or rate of return on capital. Traditional theory suggests that with only four producers and no price wars, the rate of return on capital would tend to be abnormally high in relation, say, to interest rates or to the current costs of capital. Is this in fact true? What would place a roof on excessive earnings? Would strong labor unions prevent too high rates of earnings? Or would labor and capital gang up on the consumer? And if this happened equally for *all* industries, would it make any difference, since the high money prices could be met out of high money incomes? Would competitive advertising and promotion so increase selling costs as to absorb excessive profits, keeping costs and prices in line not by reducing prices but by increasing costs? Would the threat of new entrants into a given market keep profits in bounds? And if profits were not kept in line, who would benefit from high rates of earnings, stockholders who do not control the enterprise or management that does? Also, would it be possible to maintain full employment in such an economy and avoid inflation?

An even more fundamental question is whether, in our economic model of a few great collectives, resources would be well allocated. Here we have to deal not only with the determinants of relative prices which help to guide the flow of resources into different uses but also with the direction of resources within the great collectives. It is often said that consumers direct the use of resources by what they purchase. Yet how great is consumer choice? If you want to buy a new American car this year you have, as far as I can see, very little real choice. What you are offered is a longer, heavier car with fins. I am reminded of a recent cartoon in which two men are looking down at the rear of a new high-finned car and one says to the other, "You don't like fins and I don't like fins. What would happen to the American economy if nobody liked fins?" In some ways, our big American producers are the most efficient in the world. But if finned cars are a temporary matter and are not really wanted by the people who will have to buy them second-hand, the resale value of finned cars will be low and the reduction will reflect inefficiency in the use of resources which could offset a good deal of efficiency in production. The problem of the allocation of resources through corporate enterprise is both a matter of efficiency in production and importantly a matter of what is produced. A consumer veto over wasteful use of resources is by no means the same as consumer control over their use.

Here I have raised questions about how allocation in an economy made up of big enterprises could be expected to take place. I could go a lot further in asking specific questions. But what is important here is that the questions are of a sort which cannot be answered by any amount of study of Marshallian theory, including Marshall's footnotes. Clearly a new, coherent body of allocation theory is needed if we are to understand our actual economy and make wise decisions in such matters as anti-trust policy, government regulation, and economic planning. Such a new, coherent body of theory would derive many of its parts from older theory. Other pieces for such a theory which cannot be derived from Marshallian theory are already developed or in the process of development. But, as far as I am aware, no coherent theory has been produced which would effectively describe allocation in a model economy of collective capitalism or for our actual economy, which is so largely composed of big collective corporate enterprises.

I could go on into other fields of economic theory and point to other changes in theory required by the factory system and collective capitalism: the inapplicability of the classical mechanism of international trade adjustment, the irrelevance of a wage theory which relates wage rates to the marginal product of labor, and the minor importance of a growth theory which builds on private individual invention. But to go into them would take too much space.

There is, however, one major field of theory which has been added by the development of collective capitalism and which was quite absent from traditional theory—the theory of economic planning.

Need for a Theory of Economic Planning

There has been a great deal of confusion about economic planning—particularly its relation to dictatorship. This is understandable, since economic planning has been most highly developed in the USSR and is directly tied to government operation of industry. But economic planning itself can be an important tool in a democracy. It can facilitate more effective use of resources without dictating those uses.

Consider for a moment our recent transition from a war to a postwar economy. For the first time in a long history of business fluctuations, a postwar depression was avoided. How did it happen that demand and employment were sustained after the war? Partly it was the result of the pent-up demand and monetary expansion which have always accompanied major wars. But I believe it was partly the result of economic planning (in which the Committee for Economic Development played an important role), as a result of which both government and industry were already prepared to make a quick shift from war to civilian production, and the potential goals of production were set for a full-employment economy. How this was done is a long story, but that it was done and that it did contribute to the prevention of a postwar depression, I am certain.

We find economic planning being encouraged by businessmen in connection with our foreign economic aid. Thus, one well-known business leader recently suggested that, in providing economic aid to the less-developed countries, we should require that any country to be aided should prepare a well-worked-out plan for economic development.

And, of course, we are undertaking a form of economic planning in our governmental agencies concerned with the maintenance of full employment, particularly in the Council of Economic Advisers and the Federal Reserve Board.

We also need to consider the potentials of economic planning in bringing about a better use of resources. I believe that when an adequate theory of allocation is worked out for collective capitalism, it will show a very considerable degree of indeterminacy in the allocation of resources insofar as purely economic forces are concerned, and that if we are to have a high degree of effectiveness in the use of resources and avoid the pressure for government direction, we must have a clearer picture of what seems likely to constitute effective use of resources as a background against which private, corporate, and government decisions can be made. This would be economic planning without compulsion.

Conclusion

Finally, I want to express my enthusiasm for collective capitalism. I believe that it is, to a major extent, responsible for the high levels of living which we enjoy in this country. I believe that we are still some way from understanding how it really works and what its imperatives are. We have started meeting some of these imperatives in our social security programs, in government action to clear the way for the organization of labor, and in our acceptance of government responsibility for full employment. Our problem now is to understand its operation so well that we can make it provide not only full employment and high productive efficiency but effective use of resources, equitable distribution of income, freedom to the individual to develop his resources, and the continued growth which is a potential of collective capitalism. I do not believe that this can be achieved if we base our policies on economic theories built on the postulates of Marshall's representative firm, flexible prices, and labor treated as a commodity.

As I said at the outset, I believe that our position today is very much like that of the physical scientists fifty years ago when the reality and importance of the quantum had been accepted but was not a postulate of current theories. We need an economic Niels Bohr, a de Broglie, a Heisenberg, and a Dirac to reconstruct or revolutionize economic theory as these men revolutionized physical theory. Such new theory seems to me likely to be quite different from classical theory, because so many of its underlying parts would be new. It would have to take full account of the implications of administered prices, the new status of profits, the concept of countervailing powers. I believe that such a theory would indicate the great economic and social advantages of the great corporate collectives but that it would also bring out the ways in which the economic results fall far short of being satisfactory and suggest ways in which improvement could be made. But, even more important, I believe that it would greatly clarify the character of the responsibilities which the managers of our great collectives have assumed and are only now beginning to be aware of and would provide an improved basis for public policy under our system of collective capitalism.

CHAPTER FOUR

The Reality of Administered Prices

The concept of administered prices and the importance of such prices for economic policy were first developed in a confidential memorandum to the Secretary of Agriculture in 1934. This memorandum, in preliminary form, was circulated for criticism among a number of administration economists prior to revision and publication. Information about the memorandum reached Senator William E. Borah and, apparently in the unfounded belief that it was being suppressed, the Senator introduced into the Senate and had passed a resolution demanding that the Secretary of Agriculture submit the memorandum to the Senate. This was done and the memorandum was published in January, 1935, as Senate Document #13, 74th Congress, 1st Session under the title, Industrial Prices and Their Relative Inflexibility.

This publication stirred up much discussion and controversy. By the outset of World War II, all the main conclusions of the analysis were substantially accepted except the conclusion that the inflexibility of administered prices was closely related to the degree of market concentration. Postwar discussion appears to have eliminated this source of disagreement. The two sections of the memorandum most immediately concerned with the reality of administered prices are reproduced here.

THE ATTACHED CHARTS point to the wide-spread presence in our economy of inflexible administered prices which have produced highly disrupting effects in the functioning of the economy and which are largely responsible for the failure of a policy of laissez-faire. The charts indicate that there are two essentially different types of market in operation—the traditional market in which supply and demand are equated by a flexible price and the administered market in which production and demand are equated at an inflexible administered price. In the first type of market economic adjustments are brought about primarily by fluctuations in price. In the second type of market economic adjustments are brought about primarily by changes in volume of production, while price changes are of secondary significance in producing adjustment.

The difference between market prices and administered prices is clear. A market price is one which is made in the market as the result of the interaction of buyers and sellers. The prices of wheat and cotton are market prices as are many other agricultural products. This is the type of price around which traditional economic theory has been built.

An administered price is essentially different. It is a price which is set by administrative action and held constant for a period of time [and a series of transactions]. We have an administered price when a company maintains a posted price at which it will make sales or simply has its own prices at which buyers may purchase or not as they wish. Thus, when the General Motors management sets its wholesale price for a particular model and holds that price for six months or a year the price is an administered price. Many wholesale and most retail prices are administered rather than market prices. For administered prices the price is rigid, at least for a period of time, and sales (and usually production) fluctuate with the demand at the rigid price.

Administered prices should not be confused with monopoly. The presence of administered prices does not indicate the presence of monopoly nor do market prices indicate the absence of monopoly. In many highly competitive industries, such as the automobile industry, prices are made administratively and held for fairly long periods of time. On the other hand, it is conceivable that, in a monopolized industry, the product might be turned out according to some fixed production schedule and sold for what it would bring in the market regardless of price. Thus, in the first case, we would have administered prices in a competitive industry and, in the second, market prices in a monopolized industry. In general, monopolized industries have administered prices, but so also do a great many vigorously competitive industries in which the number of competitors is small. The bulk of the administered prices shown below are in competitive industries.

CHART 4.1
RIGID AND FLEXIBLE PRICES
747 ITEMS FROM B.L.S. WHOLESALE PRICE INDEX DISTRIBUTED ACCORDING TO FREQUENCY OF PRICE CHANGE

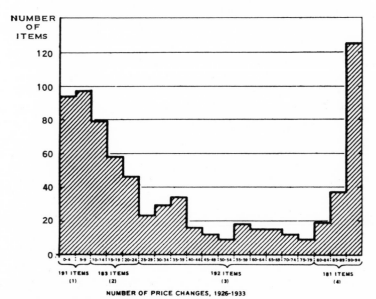

NUMBER OF PRICE CHANGES, 1926-1933

(1) CHANGED AT THE RATE OF LESS THAN ONCE EVERY 10 MONTHS.
(2) CHANGED AT THE RATE OF LESS THAN ONCE EVERY 4 MONTHS BUT MORE THAN ONCE EVERY 10 MONTHS.
(3) CHANGED AT THE RATE OF MORE THAN ONCE EVERY 4 MONTHS AND LESS THAN 3 TIMES EVERY 4 MONTHS.
(4) CHANGED AT THE RATE OF AT LEAST 3 TIMES EVERY 4 MONTHS.

Chart 4.1 indicates the very great importance of administered prices in the American economy. It shows all the commodities making up the Bureau of Labor Statistics' wholesale price index (except railroad and utility rates and a few composite items) distributed according to frequency of price change. The chart covers the number of changes from month to month for each item during the eight-year period from 1926 to 1933. In the right-hand column of the chart are 125 items which changed practically every month in the eight years. In the left-hand column are 95 items which changed price less than five times in eight years. The remaining 527 items fall between these extremes. The U-shaped character of the distribution curve carries the usual suggestion that there are two quite different types of prices. It is clear that the highly flexible prices of the right-hand group of items are for the most part made in the market, and are the type of prices around which traditional economic analysis has been built. The inflexible prices of the group of items at the left of the chart are established administratively and held for appreciable periods of time. More than half the items covered in the chart averaged less than three changes a year. These items represent a type of price essentially different in its effects from the flexible market price on which the policy of laissez-faire has been founded.

Chart 4.2 shows clearly that frequency of price change and magnitude of price change in the Depression have gone together. In this chart the same items as in Chart 4.1 are distributed along the horizontal axis according to the same scale of frequency of price change used in the first chart while the vertical scale represents the ratio of prices in 1932 to prices in 1929 taken as 100. Each dot represents one item and its distance from the base line of 100 reflects its price change between 1929 and 1932. If it is below the base line it has fallen during the Depression; if above, it has risen. At the right are the flexible priced items

CHART 4.2
RELATION BETWEEN FREQUENCY OF PRICE CHANGE AND MAGNITUDE OF PRICE CHANGE DURING DEPRESSION. DISTRIBUTION OF 750 PRICE SERIES INCLUDED IN B.L.S. WHOLESALE PRICE INDEX

BY: - FREQUENCY OF PRICE CHANGE AND MAGNITUDE OF PRICE CHANGE, -1929-1932

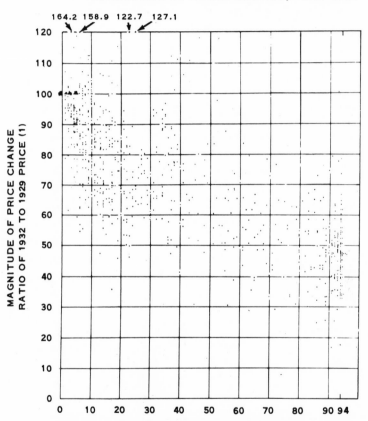

FREQUENCY OF PRICE CHANGE
NUMBER OF CHANGES IN 94 MONTHLY OPPORTUNITIES
FOR CHANGE, 1926-1933

(1) - AVERAGE OF MONTHLY PRICES

whose prices in 1932 centered around a price level half
that of 1929, while the bulk of the administered prices at
the left are centered around 90 percent of the pre-Depression levels though with a considerable dispersion. The
items which changed frequently in price show a large drop
during the Depression, while those having a low frequency
of change tended to drop only a little in price.

Chart 4.3 indicates even more clearly this tendency of

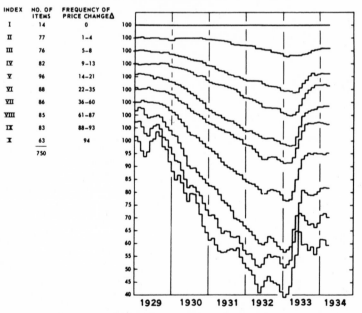

CHART 4.3

RELATION BETWEEN FREQUENCY OF PRICE
CHANGE AND MAGNITUDE OF PRICE CHANGE
DURING DEPRESSION

PRICE INDEXES FOR 750 ITEMS INCLUDED IN
B.L.S. WHOLESALE PRICE INDEX GROUPED
ACCORDING TO FREQUENCY OF PRICE
(1926-1933)[1]

INDEX	NO. OF ITEMS	FREQUENCY OF PRICE CHANGE△
I	14	0
II	77	1–4
III	76	5–8
IV	82	9–13
V	96	14–21
VI	88	22–35
VII	86	36–60
VIII	85	61–87
IX	83	88–93
X	63	94
	750	

[1] ARITHMETIC AVERAGE OF MONTHLY PRICE RELATIVES BASED
ON AVERAGE OF MONTHLY PRICES IN 1926 AS 100

△ NUMBER OF CHANGES IN 94 OPPORTUNITIES FOR CHANGE

CHART 4.4
PRICES AND PRODUCTION FOR AGRICULTURE, 1926-1933
(1926=100)

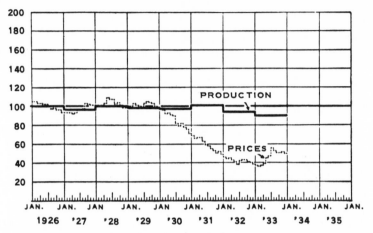

U.S. DEPARTMENT OF AGRICULTURE
BUREAU OF AGRICULTURAL ECONOMICS

frequency of price change and magnitude of price drop in the Depression to go together. It shows ten unweighted price indexes computed by grouping into one index the prices of items which did not change at all in the eight-year period; grouping in another index those which changed in price every month; and dividing the remaining items into eight groups approximately equal in number, selected and arranged according to increasing frequency of price change. Again, the big drop in price is in the items which were clearly not administered while the administered prices tended to show less price drop.

Charts 4.4 and 4.5 indicate the wholly different economic effect of flexible market prices and inflexible administered prices. Chart 4.4 shows the character of the adjustment which takes place in a market of the traditional type in which prices are flexible. It reflects the change in

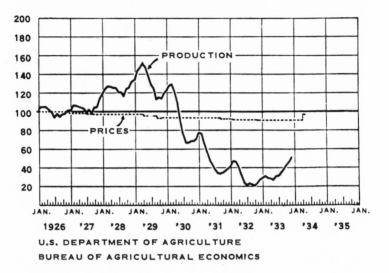

CHART 4.5
PRICES AND PRODUCTION FOR THE
AGRICULTURAL IMPLEMENTS INDUSTRY, 1926-1933
(1926=100)

U.S. DEPARTMENT OF AGRICULTURE
BUREAU OF AGRICULTURAL ECONOMICS

prices and production for agriculture as a whole during the Depression. Not until the control program in 1933 was there any significant drop in agricultural production. Practically the whole impact of falling demand worked itself out in falling prices.

Chart 4.5 shows in somewhat exaggerated form the opposite development which takes place in a market of the second type in which prices are held essentially rigid by administrative action. It reflects the changes of prices and production of agricultural implements. Practically the whole of the impact of falling demand worked itself out in falling production and only to a secondary extent by falling prices. The exaggeration comes partly from the fact that such partially counterbalancing items as improvements in quality and reduction in the direct costs of production are nowhere indicated and partly because certain minor concessions in the time payments on certain items were made, based on fluctuations in the price of certain agricultural products. Neither of these affect the essential picture told by the chart, the rigid prices and fluctuating production, which is in so much contrast to the flexible prices and stable production assumed by traditional economists and typical of the field of agriculture.

Chart 4.6 indicates the difference in economic effect of administered and market prices. It shows the relative

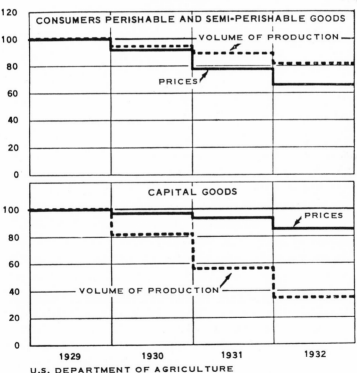

CHART 4.6
RELATIVE DECLINE IN PRICES AND PRODUCTION, 1929-1932
(1922 = 100)

U.S. DEPARTMENT OF AGRICULTURE
BUREAU OF AGRICULTURAL ECONOMICS

changes in prices and production for the consumers' perishable- and semiperishable-goods industries and the capital-goods industries. For consumers' goods, prices dropped appreciably while production dropped to a lesser extent. For the capital-goods industries, the prices dropped little while production dropped out from under the relatively inflexible prices. An important part of the difficulties in the capital-goods industries must be attributed to this fact that prices did not adjust.

Chart 4.7 indicates the disrupting effect of administered prices on the price structure. It shows the downswing of prices during the Depression and their subsequent upswing since March 1933. The indexes for the same ten commodity groups covered in Chart 4.3 are arranged in a new fashion, with time represented by the successive lines on the chart and the price relatives for different commodity groups arranged along the horizontal axis according to increasing frequency of price change. Thus, at the left are the commodity groups made up of items that changed infrequently in price. At the right are the commodity groups made up of items which changed price frequently. Each group is represented by a series of dots indicating the level of prices at successive dates with the 1929 prices as 100. Thus, the prices of group X dropped as follows: 1929, 100; January 1930, 91; January 1931, 64; January 1932, 52; January 1933, 41. For the inflexible group I, prices remained constant. For intermediate groups, the successive prices fell to intermediate degrees. Each line on the chart ties together the price relatives of the ten different commodity groups at one particular date. Thus, for January 1930, the price relatives for the ten groups lie along the second line while their price relatives for January 1933 lie along the bottom line. The progress of the Depression is shown by the general swingdown of the successive lines. The whole price structure pivoted around the rigid prices. The relative uniformity of the swingdown should be noted,

CHART 4.7

RELATIVE PRICE CHANGES FOR TEN COMMODITY GROUPS ARRANGED ACCORDING TO INCREASING FREQUENCY OF PRICE CHANGE

COMMODITY GROUPS

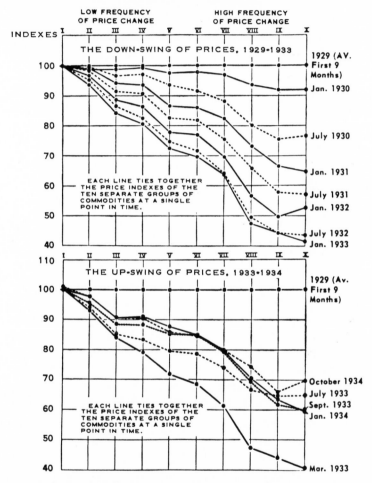

for it seems to reflect a very real set of basic price relationships. The corresponding upswing of prices since March 1933, is shown in the lower part of the chart.

If the corresponding indexes of production for each

group of items were available, they would show that the
downswing of production had pivoted around the group of
flexible priced commodities. Production at the right of the
chart would have stayed up while production at the rigid
price end of the chart would have dropped most. While
exactly corresponding production figures are not available,
the relation of price drop and production drop for 10 major
industries from 1929 to the spring of 1933 are shown
below:

	Percent drop in prices	Percent drop in production
Agricultural implements	6	80
Motor vehicles	16	80
Cement	18	65
Iron and steel	20	83
Auto tires	33	70
Textile products	45	30
Food products	49	14
Leather	50	20
Petroleum	56	20
Agricultural commodities	63	6

One can make the broad generalization, having of course
many exceptions, that for industries in which prices
dropped most during the Depression production tended to
drop least, while for those in which prices were maintained
the drop in production was usually greatest. Indeed, the
whole Depression might be described as a general dropping
of prices at the flexible end of the price scale and a dropping of production at the rigid end with intermediate effects
between.

The shift from market to administered prices reflected
in the foregoing charts is the development which has destroyed the effective functioning of the American economy
and produced the pressures which culminated in the new
economic agencies of government.

The Failure of a Laissez-Faire Policy

The whole trend of social development both in this country and abroad has been to recognize the failure of a complete laissez-faire policy.

The basic cause for the failure of a laissez-faire policy is to be found in the very same forces which have made possible a high standard of living for all, namely, the gradual, century-long shift from market to administrative coordination of economic activity which has resulted in modern industrial organization and modern technology. This shift to administration has brought a new type of competition and inflexible administered prices which disrupt the workings of the market.

A century ago the great bulk of economic activity in the United States was conducted on an atomistic basis by individuals or families—as is most of agriculture today—while the actions of the separate individuals were coordinated by the market. The individual produced for sale and his activity was geared to and in part controlled by flexible market prices. Balance between the actions of individuals was maintained—insofar as it was maintained—by the impersonal forces of the market and the law of supply and demand. Through the market, the apparently unrelated activities of individuals were thus made to mesh into a single coordinated whole and industrial policy was made by the market as a result. The policy of laissez-faire has rested on the assumption that the market would continue to make industrial policy and would remain a satisfactory coordinating mechanism.

But gradually more and more of economic coordination has been accomplished administratively. Great numbers of individuals have been drawn into large factories or business organizations and their activities have come to be coordinated within the separate enterprises by administrative action. In a single factory the separate activities of thousands of workers are coordinated by the factory management so as to mesh into a single producing organization. Within single corporate enterprises, tens and even hundreds of thousands of individuals have their economic activity coordinated by administrative direction. In 1929 the activity of over 400,000 workers was meshed into a great communication system by the management of the American Telephone & Telegraph Company. Contrast the coordination and balance among this group of workers with that among 400,000 separate farmers whose action in producing more or less of each product is controlled and balanced only by the market. In the first, we have the extreme of administrative coordination; in the second, the extreme of market coordination.

The shift from market to administrative coordination has gone so far that a major part of American economic activity is now carried on by great administrative units— our great corporations. More than half of all manufacturing activity is carried on by 200 big corporations while big corporations dominate the railroad and public-utility fields and play an important role in the fields of construction and distribution.

This development of administrative coordination has made possible tremendous increases in the efficiency of industrial production within single enterprises. The large number of workers brought into a single organization has allowed a high degree of subdivision of labor and the use of complicated series of machines so that the volume of production has been expanded way beyond the capacity of the same number of workers operating independently. Organization has made for rapid and extensive development of technology and the improving technology in turn has increased the advantages of administrative coordination. The telephone, the automobile, modern plumbing, are the joint product of technology and administration. The possibility of a high standard of living for all rests on these two interrelated factors.

But the very concentration of economic activity which brought increased productivity has by its nature destroyed the free market and disrupted the operations of the law of supply and demand in a great many industries and for the economy as a whole.

Evidence of this disruption is to be found in the administrative character and relative inflexibility of price in a great many industries and the fact that on the whole prices during the Depression have tended to go down least where the drop in demand has been greatest.

The failure of prices to adjust is perfectly familiar to business men in nearly every industry. But the implications of this familiar fact for the economy as a whole have not been recognized.

In a large part of industry, the market is not equating supply and demand through a flexible price mechanism, but is bringing an adjustment of production to demand at administratively determined prices. Thus, General Motors may set the f.o.b. price of a 1934 Chevrolet at $500 and produce the half million cars demanded at that price, yet be willing and eager to produce and sell a million cars at that price if only there were buyers.

The presence of administered prices, while it does not indicate monopoly, does mean that the number of concerns competing in the market has been reduced to the point that the individual concern has a significant power to choose within limits between changing its prices and changing its volume of production or sales. When any small drop in demand occurs, it is in a position to hold its price and reduce its production without losing all its business. As a result it tends to hold up price and reduce volume of production for the industry as a whole.

But this means that individuals have a direct power over

industrial policy which they exercise in making business policy for their own enterprise.

The distinction drawn here between industrial policy and business policy is of the greatest importance.

According to laissez-faire principles, industrial policy was supposed to result from the interaction in the market of the business policies of a large number of independent units, no one of which had any significant power. In the truly atomistic economy to which the principles of laissez-faire applied, no individual buyer or seller alone had any significant power over either price or total volume of production for the industry. Prior to The Agricultural Adjustment program, agricultural products, such as wheat and cotton, were produced and marketed under these conditions.

Where the number of competing units in a particular industry have been reduced to a relatively small handful, industrial policy is no longer made wholly by the market but in part by individuals. Industrial policy becomes subject to administrative control even though there is no monopoly or collusion between the separate enterprises.

But when the businessman has the power to affect industrial policy, he almost necessarily makes wrong industrial decisions. The very position, experience and training of the businessman which lead him to make the correct decisions on business policy tend to force him to make the wrong decisions in industrial policy in spite of the utmost public spirit which he, as an individual, may seek to exercise. The fact that his decisions are wrong from the point of view of the public interest is no necessary reflection on either his character or his intelligence, but arises from the nature of the situation within which he operates and the functions which he performs.

The businessman is expected to make business policy in a way to maximize the profits of his own enterprise. When he has the power to choose between lowering price and lowering production, good business policy frequently requires him in the presence of falling demand to hold price and curtail his production even though this means idle men and idle machines. The amount by which he can count on increasing his sales by lowering price is usually so small that the whole balance of his interest as a businessman points toward a restriction of production. The fact that he can lay off his workers enables him to cut production without having to carry the burden of idle workers as he does that of idle machines. His interest dictates lowering price only when he is able to squeeze his costs, particularly his labor costs. At best, it is an even choice whether he will choose to maintain profits or minimize losses by seeking a relatively large profit margin on a reduced volume or a small margin on a maintained volume of sales, and in such a situation the easier device, and the one involving the lesser risk, is the device of holding price and accepting curtailed volume. It is only because this holding of prices has become widespread and customary that the term "price chiseler" could be a term of opprobrium in an economy supposed to be coordinated through flexible prices.

The net effect of business control over industrial policy is, therefore, to aggravate any fluctuations in economic activity and prevent any necessary readjustments. An initial drop in demand would result, not in price readjustment, but in maintained prices and curtailment of production, thus throwing workers and machines out of employment, reducing money income and spending power, and further reducing demand. The inflexible administered prices resulting from the shift from market to administration thus act as a disrupting factor in the economy and could cause an initial small drop in demand to become a national disaster.

Only as the businessman was willing to go directly counter to the interests of his enterprise as a profit-making concern and against business tradition would he make the kind of decisions which, if made throughout industry, would keep the economy functioning and would serve the fundamental interests of business itself. If during the Depression individual businessmen throughout the economy had been persuaded to lower their prices, thus making decisions which appeared by all the standards available to them to be adverse to their interests, the result would actually have been in their interest since it would have reduced the severity of the breakdown.

So long, therefore, as concentration exists and important powers over industrial policy are exercised in the guise of business policy and result in inflexible administered prices, the market cannot be expected to coordinate and balance economic activity under a policy of laissez-faire.

Thus, administrative coordination—the very thing that has made modern technology and a high standard of living possible—has destroyed the effectiveness of the market as an overall coordinator by the inflexible administered prices which are inherent in the reduction of competing units it has produced.

It is the effects of this failure of the market mechanism which have brought the overwhelming demand from many quarters for governmental intervention in economic matters. This inflexibility has impeded the balancing of trade between nations, disrupted the workings of monetary policy, brought the banking system to its knees, obstructed the full use of human and material resources, disorganized the flow of savings into useful equipment, brought an unbalanced national budget and greatly increased economic insecurity.

The Basic Choice in Social Policy

Since the administrative coordination which promises a high standard of living carries with it inflexible administered prices which destroy the effectiveness of the market as an over-all coordinator, it is necessary to choose between two alternatives if an effectively functioning economy is to be established—either (1) atomize the administrative units to the point where inflexible administered prices disappear and the free market can become an effective coordinator, or (2) supplement the market mechanism with institutional arrangements sufficient to allow the economy to function effectively in the presence of and in spite of inflexible prices.

The first road would require the breaking up of large corporate units into a very great number of separate and wholly independent competing enterprises with the loss in efficiency which it would entail. Few realize the extent to which it would be necessary to pulverize industry. Each of the big automobile companies would probably have to be made into a hundred or more independent concerns; the big chemical companies would have to be broken into very much smaller units; and even after the break-up of the unregulated part of industry, the inflexible prices in the railroad and utility fields would impede economic adjustment, unless they also were broken up and made competitive. In order to make a laissez-faire policy truly effective, productive efficiency would have to be greatly impaired and a lower standard of living accepted than is made possible by modern industrial organization and modern technology.

The second road, while employing the market as a major instrument, would seek to supplement the market at the points where it tends to fail. Many have held that this would require Government ownership or dictatorship since they can see no other alternative to a laissez-faire policy.

Actually, the choice does not lie between private ownership and Government ownership because the problem is primarily the distribution of controls, not the locus of ownership.

Nor does the choice lie between the atomization of industry and an economic dictatorship, since it is only necessary to set up an institutional framework through which certain key industrial decisions are made and within which private or corporate enterprise and initiative can function effectively.

If inflexible administered prices are to be accepted as an inevitable product of modern technology and modern industrial organization, the following lines of action would be called for to prevent them from being a disrupting influence and to allow the optimum use of human and material resources.

First, all pressure making for a general revision of prices either upward or downward would have to be eliminated from the economy, since any development requiring a general change in the inflexible prices would result in a change in production and economic unbalance. This would mean that a monetary policy would have to be adopted which aimed to keep the flexible prices as a group approximately in line with inflexible prices as a group and that a mechanism for the adjustment of international trade balances through general changes in prices would have to be replaced.

Second, new techniques of control would have to be worked out for establishing the necessary elements of industrial policy so that the self-interest of individuals working through the market but limited by the framework of policy established would tend to produce the optimum use of human and material resources.

Finally, violent dislocation in the flow of savings into capital goods would have to be minimized.

The next three chapters are drawn from a series of statements on administrative inflation made at the request of three different Congressional committees. The first two, made before the Senate Antitrust and Monopoly Committee in July, 1957, and January, 1959, introduced the concept of administrative inflation and presented evidence of the fact of administrative inflation. The next two, submitted to the Joint Economic Committee in February, 1959, and to the Senate Antitrust and Monopoly Committee in March, 1959, examined the difference between demand inflation and administrative inflation and called attention to the lack of excess demand during the current inflation and the consequent ineffectiveness of monetary controls. The final statement made before the House Committee on Government Operations in March, 1959, sketched out a program aimed at limiting administrative inflation while reflating the economy to full employment. The body of testimony was condensed into a pamphlet, published in 1959 under the title Administrative Inflation and Public Policy, *which constitutes the following three chapters.*

CHAPTER FIVE

Administrative Inflation— 1953 to 1958

THE PARADOX OF simultaneous inflation and recession has made it apparent that a new phenomenon, unknown both to economic theory and to public policy, has arisen in American economic life.

By 1956 and early 1957, it began to be evident that the current inflation was not a product of excess demand but rather of administrative price increases. The Senate Antitrust and Monopoly Subcommittee, under the Chairmanship of Senator Kefauver, recognized this possibility and instituted hearings on Administered Prices in the summer of 1957. At the opening session on July 9, 1957, Senator Kefauver said:

> In opening these hearings on "Administered Prices," the Subcommittee on Antitrust and Monopoly is trying to come to grips with what is probably the Nation's current Number One domestic economic problem—the problem of inflation. We are concerned particularly with the extent to which administered prices in concentrated industries may contribute to this problem.

In the course of these hearings, the present author contrasted the apparent character of the new price advance that became noticeable in 1955 with the reflation from the Great Depression and with the demand inflation following World War II, saying:

> As far as I can discover this recent price rise has not been the result of excessive buying power or demand but, at least to a very considerable extent, has been a result of action within the area of discretion in which prices and wage rates

are made. This is suggested by the rise of administered prices while market prices were stable or falling.

This is a new phenomenon. I do not find it anywhere in our history of prices.

Reliable statistical data were not then available to establish the relative movement of administered and market prices in recent years, but Chart 5.1 presented the best estimate on the basis of available material. The chart showed that whereas flexible market prices had fallen more than administered prices in depression and had risen more in inflation between 1929 and 1953, the upward trend since 1955 had been in administered prices while flexible market prices remained stable. It led to the statement that

If adequate price analysis supports this conclusion . . . we have a real and immediate problem on our hands. . . . And, to me, the main problem is not to determine whether increased wage rates or increased profit margins have been more responsible, but to determine the facts as to the area of discretion and devise methods for reducing the danger that discretionary power will be used in ways harmful to the public interest.

At that time, however, it was the preponderant opinion that the inflation we were experiencing was the product of excess demand. This opinion was so strongly held that the Federal Reserve Board tightened its money policy in an effort to contract demand. This policy failed to check the inflation, but resulted instead in the depression out of which the economy has been climbing all too slowly.

Today, after experiencing the previously unheard of paradox of inflation and depression at the same time, there are few who still think that this inflation has been the product of too much demand. Clearly, the inflation has not been of the old-fashioned, classical kind with all prices rising to more or less the same extent. Rather, it is now generally understood that the new type of inflation is associated with administered prices and wage rates.

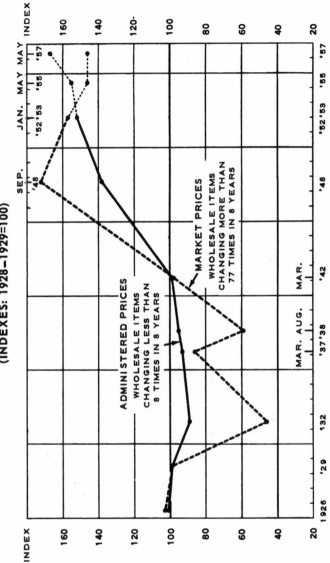

CHART 5.1
WHOLESALE PRICE BEHAVIOR
(INDEXES: 1928–1929=100)

ADMINISTERED PRICES
WHOLESALE ITEMS
CHANGING LESS THAN
8 TIMES IN 8 YEARS

MARKET PRICES
WHOLESALE ITEMS
CHANGING MORE THAN
77 TIMES IN 8 YEARS

The Nature of an Administrative Inflation

In order to understand what has happened since 1953 it is necessary to distinguish between three types of inflation. First there is the classical type of inflation in which there is too much money chasing too few goods. This is a demand or monetary inflation. There is a general agreement among economists that if you *start* with full employment, the effect of an unbalanced budget and an easy monetary policy is to generate this kind of inflation. Also there is general agreement that, under normal circumstances, a balanced budget and a tight money policy can prevent this type of inflation. This was the kind of inflation we had after the Second World War and again in the Korean War.

A second type of inflation, often called reflation, is primarily the result of the rise of market-dominated prices in a recovery from a recession or depression. Unlike a monetary inflation which is harmful, reflation is a normal and necessary part of the process of economic recovery. In a typical recession, most of the drop in prices occurs in market prices while administered prices drop much less or not at all. Then in the recovery it is appropriate for the price rise to be predominately that of market prices. This tends to restore the price balance which was distorted by the recession. Thus the rise in prices in a reflation is a constructive part of the recovery.

The third type of inflation is primarily a rise of administered prices with little rise or even a fall in market prices and is appropriately called an administrative inflation. It arises from the exercise of pricing power in concentrated industries such as steel or automobiles or from the wage pressure of strong unions. Such an administrative inflation could result from excessive wage increases or from business efforts to increase profit margins. But this kind of inflation does not come from a general excess of demand and it cannot be halted by contracting demand except by creating unemployment.

The relation between these three types of inflation should be noted. Classical inflation and reflation are, by their nature, exclusive since a classical inflation starts with full employment while reflation ends with full employment. On the other hand, an administrative inflation, because it arises from administrative power over prices and wage rates, is, in considerable measure, independent of demand, and can accompany reflation or demand inflation and can even occur when there is a general deflation in progress.

The Evidence of Administrative Inflation

The evidence of administrative inflation and its difference from a demand inflation are brought out in the four charts which follow.

Charts 5.2 and 5.3 concern the period of inflation following the Second World War and the start of the Korean War. The inflation of this period was classical in its source, with too much demand seeking too few goods. Also it was classical in its results—a more or less general lift in the price level. This can be seen in Chart 5.2 which shows the percentage increase from 1942 to 1953 in each of the commodity groups composing the Bureau of Labor Statistics Wholesale Price Index. The height of the columns shows the percentage rise of each of the major commodity groups in the index. The width of each column represents the weight that each group receives in the wholesale index, i.e., its relative importance in our economy so far as wholesale commodities are concerned. The area of each column represents the contribution that each group made to the war inflations.

The cross-hatched columns in these charts represent the commodity groups in which price administration plays a major role. For example, most of the products included

CHART 5.2
WHOLESALE PRICE CHANGES
BY PRODUCT GROUPS
1942–1953

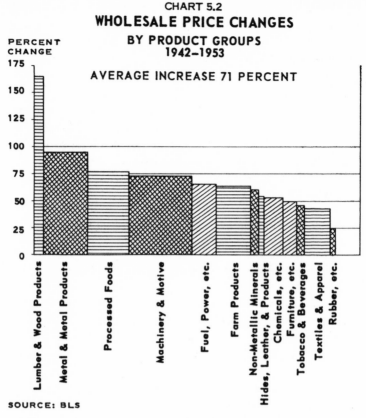

PERCENT
CHANGE

AVERAGE INCREASE 71 PERCENT

SOURCE: BLS

in Machinery and Motive Products have highly administered prices. Also in Metals and Metal Products we have mostly steel and steel products whose prices are administered. But, of course, each group includes some market-priced commodities such as steel scrap or the nonferrous metals like tin, copper, lead and zinc whose prices are really made in world markets. In spite of the fact that each group is a mixture of some administered prices and some market prices, those represented by cross-hatching —Metals and Metal Products, Machinery and Motive Products. Tobacco Manufactures and Beverages, Nonmetallic Minerals, and Rubber and Rubber Products—are

administration dominated. Similarly, the three diagonally
shaded columns for Fuel and Power, for Furniture and
Household Durables and for Chemicals and Chemical Products are intermediate mixtures, while the horizontally
shaded columns represent the highly competitive industries
such as Textile Products and Apparel, Hides and Leather
Products, Lumber and Wood Products, and, of course,
Farm Products and Processed Foods.[1]

The year 1942 has been chosen as the beginning of the
war inflations because the reflation from the Great Depression of the 1930's was not complete until then. In
1940 we had 8 million unemployed and in 1941 we still
averaged 5.5 million unemployed. By early 1942, we had
virtually full employment and the wholesale price index
had just returned to the level it had held in 1926-1929
before the Depression. The year selected as the end of the
inflation period, 1953, was two years after the peak of the
Korean War inflation had been reached and the first of
two and a half years of relative stability in the wholesale
price index. By that time, commodity prices had recovered

[1] It should be noted that two additional groups, Pulp, Paper, and
Paper Products, and Miscellaneous Products are included in Charts
5.4 and 5.5. They are not included in Charts 5.2 and 5.3 because
of lack of homogeneous series for the whole of the period covered.

The groupings used by the B.L.S. Wholesale Price Index are,
obviously, not the best possible groupings for the purpose of this
analysis. The picture would be clearer if market-dominated prices
could be separated from administration-dominated prices in each
group. Thus, it would be desirable to distinguish between the
behavior of prices for nickel and aluminum which are produced
by concentrated industries and those for copper, lead and zinc
which are influenced by a great multitude of producers for world
markets, or to distinguish within the category Processed Foods
between those foods whose prices are administration-dominated
and those which are market-dominated. If the classification were
improved, the contrast between the behavior of market and administratively controlled prices would stand out even more sharply, as
has been indicated in the analysis provided to the Senate Antitrust
and Monopoly Subcommittee by Dr. John Blair (*Hearings on
Administered Prices*, Part 10, March, 1959).

from most of the distortions arising from the process of inflation itself.

The first thing to notice in Chart 5.2 is the relatively general character of this demand inflation. With the exception of the extremes of lumber at one end and rubber at the other, there is a considerable similarity in the price movement. Seventy percent of the groups by weight rose between 49 and 77 percent. This is very much the result to be expected from a typical demand inflation. The differences in percentage increase for different groups presumably reflect the special conditions of supply and demand affecting each group, in addition to the general inflationary forces operating on all groups. Indeed these differences involve the kind of *relative* price adjustments which could be expected in an eleven year period even in the absence of inflation.

The second thing to notice in this chart is the way in which the variously shaded columns are scattered. There is no evidence here of a significant difference in the behavior of the market-dominated and the administration-dominated prices for the period as a whole. This further emphasizes the general character of this classical inflation so far as the end results are concerned.

When we look at the *process* of inflation, however, we find a quite unclassical difference in behavior between market and administration-dominated prices. In the beginning of a demand inflation, market-dominated prices tend to rise more rapidly while administration-dominated prices lag well behind. Then, in a period of readjustment, market-dominated prices fall back while administration-dominated prices continue to rise until the two groups are more nearly in balance.[2]

[2] It should be noted that there were two separate inflations between 1942 and 1953. In each case the process described above occurred. Chart 5.2 shows the combined effect of both. Chart 5.3 shows part of the first.

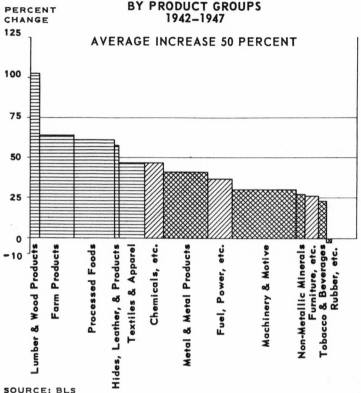

CHART 5.3
WHOLESALE PRICE CHANGES
BY PRODUCT GROUPS
1942–1947

PERCENT
CHANGE

AVERAGE INCREASE 50 PERCENT

SOURCE: BLS

The first stage in this process is shown in Chart 5.3. The chart covers the period from 1942 to 1947, but most of the rise was in the two years after the end of the war. Here we have a fairly general rise in prices but it is clearly led by prices in the highly competitive industries represented by the horizontally shaded columns. The price averages for the mixed and the administration-dominated groups represented by the diagonally shaded and the cross-hatched columns rose very much less.

Here we have the effect to be expected in a demand inflation. The excess demand had its initial impact on flexi-

CHART 5.4
WHOLESALE PRICE CHANGES
BY PRODUCT GROUPS
1953–1957

PERCENT
CHANGE

AVERAGE INCREASE 6.8 PERCENT

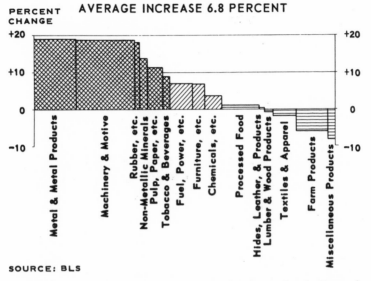

SOURCE: BLS

ble market prices, while administered prices clearly lagged behind. Thus, administration-dominated prices helped to slow up the classical inflation rather than to initiate it. Only in the later stages of this demand inflation did administered prices catch up with the general rise. This differential behavior in a demand inflation needs to be emphasized because it is so different from the differential behavior of these two groups of prices in the more recent inflation.

The contrast is apparent in Chart 5.4 which covers the inflation from 1953 to 1957, both years of fairly high economic activity. Here, clearly, the price rise has come primarily in the groups dominated by administered prices. All six administration-dominated groups, the cross-hatched columns, rose most, the three mixed groups, the diagonally shaded columns, rose to an intermediate degree and the classically competitive prices for food, leather, lumber, textiles and farm products, as groups, either went up little or actually declined. The pattern is clearly that of an administrative inflation.

Although the general wholesale price index did not begin to move upward until the first half of 1955, the year 1953 is used as the starting point for the recent inflation because there was a considerable amount of administrative inflation between 1953 and 1955 which was covered up in the wholesale price index by the fact that reflation from the 1954 depression was not complete until the middle of 1955. This is clearly shown in Table I which indicates the percent price change for the fifteen groups composing the wholesale price index from the average for 1953 to the average for the first six months of 1955. The commodity groups in bold face type correspond to the commodity groups cross-hatched in the charts and constitute the administration-dominated groups. The commodity groups in text type correspond to the commodity groups diagonally shaded in the charts and constitute the mixed groups. The commodity groups in italics correspond with the commodity groups horizontally shaded in the charts and constitute the market-dominated groups. In this 1954–1955 recession and recovery period, all six of the administration-dominated groups rose, five of them substantially while all but one of the market-dominated groups were below their 1953 level, three of them substantially. This suggests that the administrative inflation was in operation even between 1953 and the first half of 1955.

Chart 5.5 carries the analysis of the current inflation up to October 1958, but differs from the other three charts in that the category, Metals and Metal Products, has been divided into three categories—Steel, Steel Products, and Metal and Metal Products (except steel). Only the first two are given cross-hatching to represent domination by administered prices, while Metal and Metal Products (except steel) is given diagonal shading to indicate a mix-

TABLE I

WHOLESALE PRICE CHANGES
1953 TO FIRST HALF OF 1955

Commodity Groups	Percent Change
Rubber and Rubber Products	**+ 11**
Tobacco Manufactures and	
Bottled Beverages	**+ 5**
Metal and Metal Products	**+ 4**
Non-Metallic Minerals	**+ 3½**
Machinery and Motive Products	**+ 3**
Lumber and Lumber Products	+ 1½
Chemicals and Allied Products	+ 1
Pulp, Paper and Allied Products	**+ 1**
Furniture and other Household Durables	+ 1
Fuel, Power and Lighting Materials	— 1½
Processed Food	— 2
Textile Products and Apparel	— 2
Miscellaneous Products	— 4
Farm Products	— 4½
Hides, Skins, Leather and Leather Products	— 6

ture of administered prices such as aluminum and nickel and such market prices as iron and steel scrap and those of tin and other metals.

The same general pattern exists here as in the preceding chart, except that the dominating role of steel prices in this administrative inflation is clear. Not only have steel prices risen most but the steel-using machinery and motive products and other steel products have risen more than any other groups. In fact, these steel and steel using groups account for two-thirds of the gross increase in prices shown in the chart, that is, two-thirds of the area above the base line. The administered price groups, cross-hatched, account for 85 percent of the gross increase in the wholesale price index. If these groups had not gone up in price, the wholesale price index would have risen less than 1 percent and,

CHART 5.5
WHOLESALE PRICE CHANGES
BY PRODUCT GROUPS
PERCENT
CHANGE
1953 TO OCTOBER 1958

AVERAGE INCREASE 8.1 PERCENT

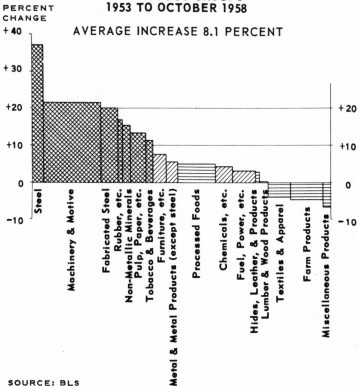

SOURCE: BLS

so far as the wholesale price index is concerned, there would have been no inflation.

The suggestion has been made that price increases during these years may represent a delayed adjustment to earlier inflationary developments and may reflect price and wage adjustments being made some time after inflationary pressures in other parts of the economy have subsided.[3] There is, however, much evidence that by 1953 the lags

[3] Testimony of Dr. Ralph Young, March 10, 1959. *Hearings on Administered Prices*, Part 10.

in wholesale price adjustment had, for the most part, been overcome.

Specifically in the case of steel, which has clearly led the rise in these years, this has not been a lagged adjustment. The following table shows indexes for finished steel prices and for the wholesale price index for certain crucial periods. The base period is the average of 1926-29, before the Great Depression. The second date is 1942, the first year in which full recovery from the Depression was achieved, and the last two are 1953 and October 1958.

TABLE II

STEEL PRICES VS. WHOLESALE PRICES

	Index of finished steel prices 1926-29=100	% change from previous period	Index of whole-sale prices 1926-29=100	% change from previous period
1926-1929	100.0		100.0	
1942	105.1	+ 5%	102.1	+ 2%
1953	210.0	+100%	175.1	+72%
October 1958	286.2	+ 36%	189.5	+ 8%

As the table shows, finished steel prices in 1942 were somewhat above their pre-Depression relation to wholesale prices, 5 percent up as compared with 2 percent for the wholesale index. From this level, steel prices doubled in the war inflation while the wholesale price index rose 72 percent. From before the big depression to 1953 the increase in steel prices was nearly 50 percent greater than the increase in wholesale prices. Thus, there is no reason to believe that the 1953 level of steel prices had failed to adjust to the new general price level. In spite of all the increases in the efficiency of steel production, the rise of steel prices from before the Depression to the present time has been more than double that of the wholesale price index. The rise from 1953 to 1958 was, very clearly, not a lag in adjustment to the previous inflation.

The differential behavior of administered and market prices stands out also during the 1958-58 recession. Table III below compares price changes from the second quarter of 1957, before the sharp recession began, to the second quarter of 1958, when industrial production reached its lowest point. The analysis is limited to industrial products since, as the President's Economic Report points out, the prices of farm and food products during this period reflect the sizable contraction in the supply of certain farm products, notably a short supply of fresh fruit and vegetables, due to bad weather conditions during the winter and spring of 1957-58 and the short supply of cattle.[4] The Metal and

[4] The index of farm prices as reported does not make it possible to distinguish between changes which reflect normal fluctuations in demand and supply and those reflecting abnormal weather conditions. In respect to demand, there is no essential difference between food and fiber and other commodities. All are subject to fluctuation in demand as incomes change and as tastes shift. But with respect to supply, most farm crops, exclusive of lumber, are subject to unplanned fluctuations due to the factor of weather, insect pests and disease. Thus the actual supply of farm products in any crop year is only partly due to the planned decisions of individual farmers. This is in direct contrast with industrial products whose output tends to be closely related to the planned output of the individual producers.

It would greatly facilitate economic analysis if price indexes for farm products could be designed which were adjusted not only seasonally, but also for weather-induced abnormalities in supply.

As it is, it is necessary to keep the possibility of such abnormalities in mind when farm products are included in the inflation analysis. The prices of Farm Products, Processed Foods and Miscellaneous Products whose principal item is animal protein feeds have been excluded from the analysis of the period 1957-58 because of the freezes in the winter of 1957-58 which greatly curtailed the supply of fresh fruits and vegetables and because of the abnormally low supply of cattle as farmers were induced by high cattle prices to hold back heifer calves to add to their breeding herds, thereby further pushing up the price.

Farm Products, Processed Foods, and Miscellaneous have been included in Charts 5.4 and 5.5, however, because there is no evi-

Metal Products group has been divided as in Chart 5.5 and Miscellaneous has been treated as farm and food because it is dominated by animal protein feeds. As in Table I, the bold face type of Table III indicates the administration-dominated groups, the text type indicates the mixed groups, and italic type indicates the market-dominated groups.

TABLE III
WHOLESALE PRICE CHANGES
SECOND QUARTER 1957 to SECOND QUARTER 1958

Commodity Groups	Percent Change
Semifinished and Finished Steel	+ 4.1
Machinery and Motive Products	+ 3.0
Tobacco Manufactures and Bottled Beverages	+ 2.7
Fabricated Steel	+ 2.7
Furniture and Other Household Durables	+ 1.4
Pulp, Paper and Allied Products	+ 1.3
Chemicals and Allied Products	+ 1.2
Hides, Skins, Leather and Leather Products	+ .9
Non-Metallic Minerals	+ .3
Rubber and Rubber Products	− .4
Textile Products and Apparel	− 2.0
Lumber and Wood Products	− 3.2
Fuel, Power and Lighting Materials	− 6.7
Metal and Metal Products (ex. steel)	− 9.9
Farm Products	+ 7.8
Miscellaneous	+ 7.2
Processed Foods	+ 7.8

dence that abnormalities in supply significantly affect the before-and-after comparison of 1953 with 1957 or with October 1958 which cover a span of four or more years and a change in the wholesale price index of 6.8 percent or more.

This abnormality in farm and food products is much less serious when longer periods and large changes in the average of prices are examined. It becomes acute when a short range and small change comparison is made. The 1957-58 comparison covers changes in a single year and a change in the wholesale price index of less than 1.8 percent.

During this year of recession the industrial price *average* was very stable. But this stability of the industrial price index was a product of two opposite and offsetting developments. The price indexes of all but one of the administration-dominated groups rose, five of the seven by substantial amounts, while most of the market-dominated and mixed groups fell. Even the administration-dominated group which failed to rise, that of rubber, helps to confirm the general picture when the market priced natural rubber, which dropped 22 percent, is separated from the administration-dominated rubber products which rose 2 percent. For industrial prices as a whole, the continued administrative inflation was *masked* by deflation of market-dominated prices. Thus inflation and deflation combined to give a false appearance of price stability.

In the partial reflation period since the spring of 1958 the administrative inflation appears to have continued along with some reflation of market-dominated industrial prices, a compound movement which has been masked in the wholesale price index by the offsetting fall in the indexes of farm and food products as the particular scarcities of that spring have disappeared.

In the light of all this evidence, anyone who thinks that the recent inflation is not an administrative inflation had better study the record.

The Absence of Demand Inflation

Since administrative inflation and demand inflation can occur simultaneously, the question still remains as to whether or not there was demand inflation at any time since 1953. Actually, there is no evidence of excess demand during this period. This becomes clear from an analysis of the relation between demand and capacity during these five years.

First, it is important to note that 1953 was a year of high employment without inflationary pressures. Unemployment in 1953 averaged less than 1.9 million, following two years of almost equally low unemployment. Thus, the Economic Report of the President stated in January 1954, "Perhaps never before in their history have the American people come closer to realizing the ideal of high and expanding employment, without price inflation, than in 1953."[5]

From 1951 to the beginning of 1953 some measure of price control had been in effect. However, the inflationary pressure of the Korean War had subsided so that by January 1953 the wholesale price index was 6 percent below its 1951 peak. As a result, when price controls were finally dropped in early February 1953 there was no rise in prices. As the President's Economic Report stated, "The removal of controls early in February 1953 had apparently as little effect on the year's wage movements as on its price developments."[6]

Let us then examine the relation of production to capacity in recent years, using 1953 as a non-inflationary, full-employment base.

First consider unemployment after 1953. In every year since 1953 unemployment has averaged close to a million more than in 1953.[7] The same excessive unemployment is

[5] *Economic Report of the President*, Transmitted to the Congress January 28, 1954. U. S. Government Printing Office, Washington, 1954, p. 11. It is perhaps ironic that at the time the President's Report was written, the recession leading to the 1954 depression was already in evidence since the seasonally adjusted index of industrial production had been declining for four successive months and unemployment had been increasing more than seasonally for four months. By December, 1953, employment was half a million less than in December, 1952, and industrial production, seasonally adjusted, was down five points from the beginning of the year. Growth had stopped in the summer of 1953.
[6] *Ibid.*, p. 39.
[7] Unemployment came within 952,000 of the 1953 figure in 1956, but was over one million in every other year since 1953 (all figures employ the new definitions of unemployment). It should be noted that the picture would be even more striking if only the first

shown quarter by quarter. In each quarter since 1953, un-, employment has been more than 850,000 higher than in the lowest quarter of 1953. In other words, *in no quarter since 1953, a year without inflationary pressure, has demand been pressing on the labor supply.*

The same conclusion applies to manufacturing capacity. This can be seen in Chart 5.6 which presents indexes of manufacturing capacity and production since 1953.[8] As can be seen from the chart, manufacturing capacity expanded faster than production so that, at the successive peaks of production, demand was less and less pressing on capacity. Indeed, at the peak quarter in 1955, manufacturing production was only 6 percent over its peak quarter in 1953, while capacity had increased by 16 percent in the same period. And after 1955, while manufacturing capacity continued to expand at much the same rate, there was no significant increase in production. *This is certainly not a picture of demand pressing on capacity.* And if there was no demand inflation in 1953, how could there be demand inflation in 1955 or later when both labor and manufacturing capacity were less fully used?

It has been suggested that the inflation came in response to a high demand for durable goods, so let us look at the record there. Since it is well known that durable goods capacity has expanded more rapidly than total manufacturing capacity, the latter has been used as a conservative measure of the growth of durable goods capacity. As can be seen in Chart 5.7, there is very much the same pattern

eight months of 1953 were used as the full-employment, noninflationary base, since unemployment in the first eight months, seasonally adjusted, was less than for the year as a whole because of the recession in the last four months.

[8] Derived from the *Economic Report of the President*, January 20, 1959, p. 11. Chart 5.6 differs from that published in the Economic Report in one respect. The December 31, 1952, value for capacity is taken as 100 instead of December 31, 1953, since obviously capacity was at least as great in early 1953 as output.

CHART 5.6
MANUFACTURING CAPACITY AND PRODUCTION

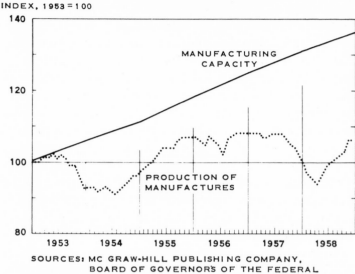

INDEX, 1953 = 100

SOURCES: MC GRAW-HILL PUBLISHING COMPANY,
BOARD OF GOVERNORS OF THE FEDERAL
RESERVE SYSTEM.

for durable goods as for manufacturing as a whole. Here, too, production lags way behind the build-up of capacity. Again evidence of demand pressing on capacity is lacking. Rather, after 1955 we have the picture of mild stagnation, recession, and partial recovery.

But what of steel which was such an important contributor to the price rise after 1953? Chart 5.8 shows the relation of steel capacity and output. In spite of the heavy production of autos and other durable goods, steel production in 1955 did not come as close to capacity as in the first half of 1953. Only in the spring and fall of 1956 did steel production reach rated capacity. This, however, can scarcely be regarded as an example of excess demand. It was, rather, a reaction to the six weeks' strike which occurred in the summer of 1956. It is well recognized that when a strike is possible on a certain date inventories are

CHART 5.7
OUTPUT OF DURABLE MANUFACTURES
F.R. INDEXES, ADJUSTED FOR SEASONAL VARIATION, 1947–49=100

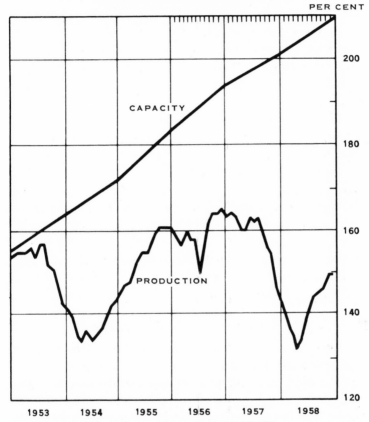

SOURCES: MC GRAW-HILL PUBLISHING COMPANY,
BOARD OF GOVERNORS OF THE FEDERAL
RESERVE SYSTEM.

built up ahead of time, as happened again in the spring of 1959, and are then depleted during the strike and rebuilt after it is over.

The fact that the high rate of steel production in the spring and fall of 1956 was not a product of excess demand but of a temporary deficiency in production during the summer is indicated by the horizontal dotted line of Chart 5.8 which represents the average demand for 1956 and is well below the levels of 1953 and 1955. Thus, there was no excess of demand for steel after 1953 of a sort which could be thought of as part of a demand inflation. Rather, steel prices showed a tendency to rise without respect to demand. Whether market prices were falling with a fall in general demand or were rising with a rise in general demand, steel prices moved up year by year. Chart 5.9 shows steel prices rising in every year since 1953 and it is not possible from a study of the chart to determine which were years of recession and falling demand and which years of higher demand.

Clearly, so far as wholesale prices are concerned, the dominant fact of the inflation since 1953 has been its administrative character. At no time since 1953 has demand been pressing on either the labor supply or manufacturing capacity as strongly as it did in 1953 when there was no demand inflation. Indeed, after 1953 *there was not even sufficient demand to produce full employment, let alone generate demand inflation.*

The Source of Administrative Inflation

Once the fact of administrative inflation is accepted, the next problem is to discover its source. Business management calls it wage inflation and blames the unions. Labor points to the pricing power of management and says this power has been abused. In theory, an administrative inflation could arise either from labor seeking to push up wage rates faster than productivity or from management seeking to increase profit margins too much, or from a combination of these two. What are the facts?

An examination of the situation in steel will throw some light on the question. To focus on steel prices seems appropriate, not only because steel is a kingpin in the administrative inflation, but because steel is a kingpin in our whole

CHART 5.8

STEEL CAPACITY AND PRODUCTION

(INGOTS AND STEEL FOR CASTINGS)

INDEX, 1947-49 = 100

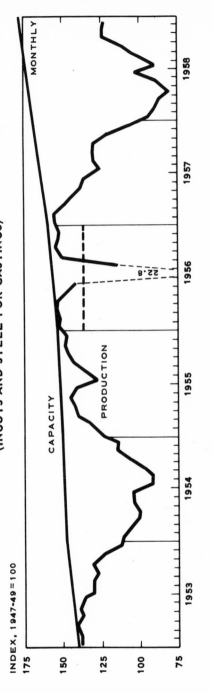

CHART 5.9

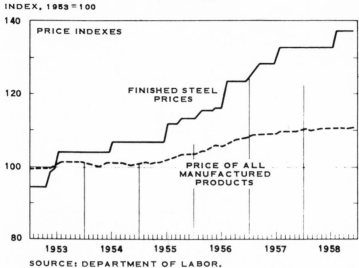

SOURCE: DEPARTMENT OF LABOR.

economy, with its price effects ramifying in all directions. Materials presented to the Senate Antitrust and Monopoly Subcommittee by the steel companies and the steelworkers' union provide a basis for answering the question: what is the source of the increase in steel prices?

As far as the increase during the demand inflation resulting from the two wars is concerned, neither labor nor management was responsible. Careful analysis of the data introduced by management shows that both the employment costs per ton in producing steel and the prices of steel lagged well behind the general price rise until the last stages of the war inflations. During most of this period, wage rates went up less quickly than the increases in productivity and in cost of living would justify and by 1953 they had hardly caught up with the general rise in the price level. As Chart 5.3 shows, prices of metals and metal products, predominantly steel, showed a smaller rise in price from 1942 to 1947, the early part of the inflation period, than did prices in the more competitive industries.

Thus, the restrained behavior of both labor and management operated to slow down the inflation which arose from excess demand.

The administrative inflation since 1953 is quite a different matter, for as we have seen steel has been leading, not lagging behind, the price increases in other industries.

In the Senate Subcommittee Hearings in the summer of 1957, a great deal of attention was focused on the average $6 increase in the prices of finished steel which took place in July of that year. On this, Mr. Roger W. Blough, Chairman of the Board, United States Steel Corporation, testified as follows:

> In our most recent negotiations last year—after a five-week strike—we signed a labor agreement. It was that labor agreement which foreordained our recent price increase. On July first of this year we faced what our recent total wage-cost history demonstrates was about a six and a half percent increase in our total costs per man-hour; and to cover these costs in part, we raised our steel prices by an average of four percent.[9]

There are three points to notice about this placing of the entire blame for these price increases on the labor contract.

First, the statement of costs is in terms of cost *per man-hour,* not in terms of cost *per ton.* At no point in the formal presentation by the company was the effect of the increase in output per man-hour considered or the net effect of the wage increase on cost per ton discussed. And, of course, it is cost per ton and not cost per hour which is important for pricing.

Second, Mr. Blough's 6½ percent increase due to the labor contract includes not only the increase in employment cost expected, but also the expected increase in the cost of purchased materials and services *per man-hour of*

[9] Hearings on Administered Prices, Part 2, p. 211.

employment. The company argued that historically, when their employment cost per man-hour went up $1 their total costs—including both employment cost and cost for purchased raw materials, fuel and services—went up more than $2.[10]

This is more or less what one would expect as a result of a demand inflation when everything goes up by more or less the same amount. But it would not necessarily follow in an administrative inflation. What is immediately important is that the corporation reasoned that since employment cost per man-hour was going up nearly 6 percent, total costs divided by total man-hours could be expected to go up 6½ percent.

The third thing to notice is that there is no reference to the changes in steel prices since the previous adjustment of steel wages to productivity in the summer of 1956. Yet finished steel prices had been increased an average of $5 a ton during the winter of 1956-57, primarily through increasing steel extras. Also a three-cent cost-of-living increase was required by the labor contract in the same period. Both of these increases need to be included if we are to appraise Mr. Blough's conclusion that the labor contract forced the $6 increase in steel prices in July 1957. We can restate the problem: *Did the increased cost per ton of steel resulting from the labor contract, including both the cost-of-living increase in the winter and the July 1 increases, justify an $11 increase in steel prices?*

A careful analysis by the present author of the data presented in the Hearings leads to the conclusion that the increase in labor costs per ton *due to the labor contract* was not more than $1.75 per ton.[11] Also, the cost of mate-

---

[10] *Ibid.*, p. 244.

[11] The exact method of arriving at this conclusion is set forth in detail in the *Hearings on Administered Prices*, Part 9, pp. 4762-4766. Examination of the data presented by management and labor at the Steel Hearings (*Ibid.*, parts 2, 3 and 4) disclosed much greater agreement on the increases in cost *per man-hour* than some

rials and services per ton appears to have gone down in this period. Thus, only a small proportion of the $11 per ton price increase can be attributed either directly or indirectly to the labor contract.

A similar conclusion is reached with respect to the role of labor in relation to the administrative inflation if we examine the increases in wage rates and productivity, not in steel alone but in manufacturing as a whole. From 1953 to 1957, hourly earnings of factory workers increased an average of 17 percent.[12] If output per factory worker had also increased 17 percent as a result of technical improvement, there would, on the average, have been no increase in wage costs per unit of product and so no basis for price increases. On the basis of studies covering the years from 1953 to 1956[13] and evidence of continued technical improvement in the following years the output per man-hour from 1953 to 1957 appears to have increased approximately 16 percent from technical progress.[14] This would leave only a one percent increase in the labor cost per unit due to the increase in hourly wages of factory workers. Of

---

of the statements at the hearings suggested. The major difference in the respective figures on costs *per ton* arose from the fact that labor adjusted the increase in costs per man-hour under the contract from mid-1956 to mid-1957 for the estimated increase in output per man-hour due to technical improvement in the same period. Management took no account of this factor and treated the increase in cost per hour for the contract year as if it were identical with the increased cost per ton for the period. The above calculation of $1.75, of course, takes account of increased output per man-hour.

[12] *Economic Report of the President*, January 1959, p. 169. Average gross hourly earnings of all manufacturing workers.

[13] Joint Economic Committee, *Productivity, Prices and Incomes*, Washington, 1957, p. 89.

[14] It should be noted that the actual figures of output per man-hour published by the B.L.S. show a lower increase from 1953 to 1957. These figures reflect both the increase in output per hour due to improved technology and also the decline in output per hour due to the lower rate of operation in 1957 as compared with 1953.

course, the salaries of non-factory workers may have increased faster than their output. But as far as production workers are concerned, only a small part of the 10 percent increase in industrial prices between 1953 and 1957 can properly be attributed to the increase in wage rates.

Whether the rest of the 10 percent increase in industrial prices can be justified on other grounds is another matter. Management points to the effect of inflation on depreciation charges when accounting is based on historical cost. However, it is difficult to believe that even a full account of these effects would justify the whole of the price increases. The U. S. Steel Corporation itself, in its testimony before the Senate Subcommittee, treated the accounting effects of inflation as a secondary factor.

Consider specifically the $11 increase in steel prices in 1956-57. If $1.75, or even $2.00, could be justly attributed to an increase in labor costs, how much of the remainder was an increase in profits? This question cannot be answered simply, because the recession immediately followed the June 1957 wage increases. Steel profits dropped, partly because of the big drop in steel sales and partly because of increased unit costs due to the large amount of overhead labor required in the making and selling of steel which has to be spread over a smaller amount of production.[15] The very high rates of steel profits in the first quarter of 1959, when the volume of sales had recovered, suggest that an important part of the price increases of 1957 and 1958 went to widen profit margins.

We thus appear to have a clear case in steel, not only of the existence of an important degree of pricing discretion, but of the exercise of that power to increase prices signifi-

---

[15] Quite apart from non-production workers, when steel is operating at an average rate close to a fifth of the production workers are "overhead." As a result, when production falls, the man-hours of production work do not fall in the same proportion and output per production worker declines.

cantly in excess of the increase justified by increased costs.

Moreover, since the steel industry, a leader in the administrative inflation, tried to place prime responsibility on labor where it clearly does not belong, and since, in manufacturing as a whole, prices since 1953 were raised very much more than would seem to be justified by the effect on costs of increased wage rates adjusted for increased productivity, there should be great hesitancy in accepting the widespread contention of management that labor is to a major extent the source of this administrative inflation.

CHAPTER SIX

Monetary Policy and Administrative Inflation

IN THE PAST, a tight money policy has been regarded as a major instrument for controlling inflation. Also, an easy money policy has come to be regarded as a device to stimulate demand when unemployment is excessive. However, there is an obvious conflict in traditional policy when inflation and unemployment occur together. In order to find a possible way out of this conflict, we need to examine both the theory and the practice of monetary policy.

Monetary Policy and Demand—1953 to 1959

It is generally agreed among economists that insofar as monetary measures operate on inflation and employment they do so through influencing the demand for goods. However, there is not general agreement as to the extent to which monetary measures can, in fact, influence demand. Most economists agree that a tight money policy can restrict demand and, under normal circumstances, can prevent a demand inflation. But there is greater uncertainty as to the effectiveness of an easy money policy in expanding demand. Some economists hold that an easy money policy and expansion in the money supply cannot bring about an expansion of demand. Others hold, with John Maynard Keynes, that an easy money policy can stimulate demand when interest rates are high, since a reduction in rates will stimulate investment, but that once rates have been reduced to a minimum level, further monetary expansion will have no further stimulating effect. A third group holds that monetary expansion can stimulate demand both through reducing interest rates and also directly, so that even when interest rates are at a minimum, further monetary expansion will bring added demand.[1]

It appears to be the position of the Federal Reserve Board that a tight money policy can limit demand and that an easy money policy can induce an expansion of demand.[2] This is the position which will be adopted here. It means that a tight money policy can be an effective instrument for controlling a demand inflation and an easy money policy can be an effective instrument for increasing demand when there is excessive unemployment. On the other hand, there is nothing in this theory which indicates that monetary measures can control an administrative inflation without creating excessive unemployment. Let us, then, examine monetary policy and its effects since 1953.

A rough measure of monetary policy and its effect on the real money supply and the level of industrial production are given in Chart 6.1. The step-like line represents the discount rate of the New York Federal Reserve Bank which is a fairly accurate reflection of that much more complex thing, Federal Reserve Policy—the central monetary policy of the country. The lower, fluctuating line represents the changes in the real money supply which result from monetary policy.[3] The top line shows the fluctuations of industrial production.

[1] This view holds that Keynes' liquidity trap can operate, so far as loans are concerned, when interest rates are so low that individuals and enterprises would prefer to hold any amount of money rather than make additional loans; but that there would seem to be no point short of satiety at which individuals and enterprises would prefer to hold any amount of money rather than purchase more goods or services for consumption or investment.

[2] Cf. *The Monetary System of the United States*, by Dr. Ralph A. Young, Federal Reserve Bulletin, February, 1953.

[3] The measure of the real money supply is derived by dividing the monthly figures for "adjusted demand deposits and currency" by the consumer price index. A more refined deflator for the money series could be devised but the actual result would not be significantly different. The real money supply is stated in terms of 1958 prices.

CHART 6.1
INDUSTRIAL PRODUCTION, DISCOUNT RATE AND REAL MONEY SUPPLY
SEASONALLY ADJUSTED

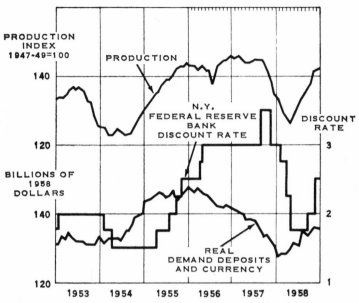

SOURCES: BOARD OF GOVERNORS OF THE FEDERAL RESERVE SYSTEM. DEPARTMENT OF LABOR.

As can be seen from Chart 6.1, there was neither a tight nor an easy money policy in 1953 and some monetary expansion occurred in the first part of the year. In early 1954, an easy money policy was adopted to increase demand and help overcome the 1954 recession with a $10 billion expansion in the real money supply. The easy money policy was reversed in the late spring and summer of 1955, bringing to a virtual halt the expansion in the real money supply. Then, in the fall of 1955, a tight money policy was instituted which was further tightened in 1956 and kept tight through 1957 and the first quarter of 1958. From the spring of 1956, the effect of this policy was to produce a fairly steady contraction in real money supply amounting to over $17 billion by the beginning of 1958. In the spring of 1958, the tightness in money policy was relaxed but real money expansion did not begin until an easy money policy was adopted in April 1958 with a consequent expansion of more than $5 billion in the real money supply. This monetary expansion was brought to a halt in early November 1958 when the money policy was again tightened.

Just what was the effect on inflation of the tight money policy from late 1955 to early 1958? In late 1955 and early 1956, it may well have served to prevent a demand inflation which would otherwise have occurred, although demand, in fact, did not rise to the extent required for full employment. In the latter part of 1955, there was a high demand for credit, partly to finance the heavy volume of auto purchases and partly to finance capital expansion by business. This tended to lift interest rates above their 1953 levels and this might have resulted in some demand inflation if expansion in the real money supply had not been limited.[4] However, this action did not prevent administrative inflation.

After early 1956 the situation was quite different. By the spring of 1956 manufacturing demand was easing off, particularly for durable goods other than steel, which was being accumulated in anticipation of a strike. As we have seen, at no time after the spring of 1956 was demand sufficient to push manufacturing production significantly above its highest 1955 level in spite of surplus labor and productive capacity. The further tightening of monetary policy after the spring of 1956 was thus effective in limiting

[4] An excess in demand could have been expected because, with higher short term interest rates, the public, and particularly those in touch with the short-term loan markets, would have wanted to hold smaller money balances, keeping a larger proportion of their liquid assets in an interest-earning form.

demand. But, because there was no initial excess in demand, the further tightening of policy inhibited growth in the presence of unused resources, while administrative inflation continued.

Then, in the summer of 1957, when there were ample signs that demand was steadily weakening relative to normal growth, the extreme tightening of money was a shock to the business community that could well have initiated the sharp recession which followed and, along with the previous tightening, have been its primary cause. The recession brought a fall in market prices which masked the continued administrative inflation but did not halt it.

The conclusion seems inescapable that a tight monetary policy cannot stop administrative inflation without creating excessive unemployment, and may not be able to do so even then. In the last three years, the effort to control administrative inflation by a tight money policy appears to have cost the nation at least $70 billion of national production (at 1958 prices) which would have been available if demand had not been so curbed by the tight money policy that a significant amount of manpower and industrial capacity was idle. Whether the administrative inflation during the period would have been greater if a full-employment monetary policy had been pursued is open to debate.

It is easy to see why the Federal Reserve Board continued its tight money policy after the spring of 1956. The wholesale price index continued to rise and the consumer price index began to rise in the summer of 1956. In traditional economic theory, rising prices are an indication of excess demand. An undiscriminating analysis of price movements seemed to confirm the general character of the inflation. And the concept of an administrative inflation was not then current.[5]

[5] The term "administrative inflation" was first used and the concept spelled out in the author's testimony before the Senate Antitrust and Monopoly Subcommittee in July 1957 and evidence was

However, suppose that the Federal Reserve Board had been given an analysis showing that after the spring of 1956 there was no demand inflation, that neither labor nor plant capacity was being fully utilized, and that administrative inflation was under way. Consider the dilemma which would have faced the Board: Should demand be expanded so as to bring about full employment while administrative inflation continued; or should demand be contracted in an effort to prevent administrative inflation even though this meant excessive unemployment? This would have been an awful choice and there is a good deal of question whether such a momentous decision should rest with the Federal Reserve Board.

Recognition of the Ineffectiveness of Monetary Measures to Control Administrative Inflation

By March 1959 it was coming to be widely recognized that the inflation was administrative in character and that a tight money policy was powerless to deal with it. On March 12, the economic advisor to the Federal Reserve Board, Dr. Woodlief Thomas, stated in a letter to the *Washington Post:*

> Recent discussion of the influence of administered prices, stimulated by . . . the Kefauver Committee, . . . has made a significant contribution to a better understanding of the problems of inflation and fluctuations in economic activity and employment. This contribution is in pointing out that there are unstabilizing forces in pricing actions of the private economy—on the part of both management and labor—that cannot be effectively controlled or corrected by governmental actions in the area of fiscal and monetary policies.

Dr. Thomas concluded that "much of the unemployment existing today can be attributed to distortions and inflexi-

---

presented there suggesting that the current inflation was administrative in character. *Hearings on Administrative Prices,* Part 1, p. 84.

bilities in the price and income structure." Essentially this same position was taken by the Chairman of the President's Council of Economic Advisors, Raymond J. Saulnier, who wrote, "In my judgment these price increases [in the heavy industries and consumer durables] were a major factor in limiting demand and thereby restraining output."[6] A similar position was taken by Dr. Ralph Young, Director of the Division of Research and Statistics of the Federal Reserve Board, in testimony before the Kefauver Committee on March 10, 1959.

On March 14, *The New York Times* carried an editorial on the same subject entitled "An Aroused Reserve Board." This editorial described the "extremely serious dilemma . . . presented to the monetary authorities" by the new type of inflation. The editorial pointed out that "general credit controls are too blunt an instrument for dealing with this type of price rise. If applied with sufficient vigor they can slow down the whole economy and produce widespread disemployment, thus creating the impression that the Federal Reserve Board was neglecting its responsibilities under the Employment Act of 1946." Further the editorial says of the Board "that a point has certainly been reached when it finds itself forced into the position of 'taking the rap' for inflationary policies that are socially and economically unsupportable, but with which it is not equipped to deal."

The same subject was also discussed in a *Washington Post* editorial under the title, "The Price Issue Is Joined."[7] This editorial said, "There is a growing consensus that present fiscal and monetary controls of the Government simply cannot cope with the administered price sector of the economy where concentrated industries like steel can, as they have shown, defy sagging demand, increase prices

[6] In a letter to Representative Thomas B. Curtis, dated February 18, 1959 and made public on March 9 by the Joint Economic Committee.
[7] March 12, 1959.

and profits and thus seriously retard economic growth."
The editorial closed with the following words:

So the issue is joined. If the makers of steel and autos and
other heavy manufacturing and the unions which serve these
industries will now acknowledge their power, accept the social
responsibility that goes with it and discharge it in the public
interest, the American economy can avoid further regimenta-
tion and control. If they will not Congress and the Administration will be under mounting pressure to devise effective
restraints.

CHAPTER SEVEN

Full Employment without Inflation

The Dilemma of Business and Lagging Employment

AT THE BEGINNING of 1959, President Eisenhower said in his Economic Report, "We may justifiably take satisfaction in the increases already achieved in employment, production, and incomes and in the fact that the·price level has been reasonably steady of late."[1] In commenting on the economic prospects, he stated, "As 1959 opens, there is reason for confidence that the improvement in business activity which began in the second quarter of last year will be extended into the months ahead."[2]

These statements confuse the recovery of business with the recovery of employment. From the bottom month of the recession, the increase in employment had hardly kept pace with the increase in the labor force and the formal figures for unemployment were higher in January 1959 than a year earlier. Even after the increase of 1.1 million in employment in March, a large part of which was a seasonal increase, employment had increased over the preceding March by only half a million more than the normal increase in the labor force. Though business was back to pre-recession levels, little progress had been made toward fuller employment.

The small progress toward full employment stands out more clearly when we examine the increase in jobs which would be needed to achieve reasonably full employment. In 1953, the most recent year of full employment, unem-

[1] *Economic Report of the President*, 1959, p. 4.
[2] *Ibid.*, p. iv.

ployment averaged appreciably less than two million. Therefore, the goal of not more than two million unemployed seems a reasonable goal for full employment. To reach this goal from the March 1959 level of over four million unemployed would require much more than an increase of two million jobs. When demand is expanded, additional labor is drawn into employment not only from those listed as unemployed but also from three other major sources.

The first is the expansion in the labor force itself. With jobs not so plentiful, the labor force has not maintained its normal rate of growth. When jobs are scarce, people on the borderline of wanting jobs drop out of the labor force, older individuals approaching retirement who lose their jobs do not seek others, and in other ways people who really want to work are not looking for work and so officially drop out of the labor force. Plentiful job opportunities bring these people back into the body of productive workers, adding to their own welfare and to that of the nation. As much as a million extra workers might come from this source.

A second source of additional non-agricultural workers consists of those who would leave agriculture, once non-farm jobs were plentiful. In the last five years of somewhat reduced job opportunities, the flow of workers off the farm has been at half the rate of the preceding five years, a difference of more than half a million. How much of this slowdown is due to reduced job opportunities is hard to determine, but a considerable part can be attributed to this source.

Finally, the involuntary part-time workers provide an added source of labor and full-time workers are likely to put in an increased amount of overtime as demand increases to the full-employment level. An increase in the work-week could easily add the equivalent of another million full-time workers.

These three sources of manpower might easily add the equivalent of two million workers. In that case, with over four million now unemployed, it would require the equivalent of more than four million additional full-time jobs outside of agriculture, plus the jobs necessary to absorb the normal addition to the labor force, in order to reduce unemployment to the figure of two million. Thus, if job expansion continued only at the rate which existed from March 1958 to March 1959, it would take something like four or five years to achieve a level of full employment comparable to 1953.[3]

Is this rate of job expansion likely to continue? By the spring of 1959, two of the major sources of recovery had lost much of their immediate potency and a third was no longer being employed. The reversal of the inventory contraction which accompanies a recession is a strong factor in recovery, once the turning point has been reached, but a large part of the recovery impetus from this source had already spent itself. Also, the heavy government spending and deficit which contributed to the partial recovery appeared likely to diminish greatly by summer. And the easy money policy adopted in the spring and summer of 1958, which brought a $5 billion expansion in the money supply in the nine months from February to November, was reversed in the fall of 1958. With these three stimulating factors not operating strongly, even the slow rate of absorption of the unemployed might not continue without some new stimulus such as that of an easier money policy.

This brings us back to the dilemma in monetary policy created by administrative inflation. An easier money policy

[3] Civilian employment in March 1959 was 63.828 million, 1.517 million more than in March 1958. If the normal growth in the labor force is taken as 800,000, only 717,000 of the jobs went to reduce unemployment. Also the big increase in employment in April 1959 was partly seasonal and partly due to an excessive increase in steel, auto, and other inventories as insurance against a steel strike.

to stimulate employment would not only raise market prices by expanding demand, but would also, in part, validate the administrative inflation which has already taken place and lay the basis for further administrative inflation. On the other hand, if the price indexes are to be kept stable while administrative inflation continues, a tight money policy would be needed which would so limit demand that market-dominated prices would drop enough to offset and mask the rise of administration-dominated prices. This policy would maintain or increase the excessive unemployment, just as happened between the second quarter of 1957 and the second quarter of 1958. In one case, we would have continued inflation, with the damage it does to those with fixed incomes, pensions and the like; in the other case, we would have continued depression while the burden of price stability would be placed on the small business man, the farmer and the unemployed.

Some people have suggested that, because of the conditions leading to administrative inflation, we have to choose between the two horns of the monetary dilemma. Certainly, if the whole matter were left to monetary action, this would appear to be the case.

However, these are not the only alternatives if we are willing to go outside of the field of monetary policy. The view of this author is that it is well within our power to develop a program which will bring about full employment with a reasonably stable price level, and at the same time retain the advantages of the free enterprise system. Such a program is outlined in the following section.

An Immediate Program for Recovery

So far as the immediate future is concerned, the problem is to hold down administration-dominated prices while we reflate to full employment through an easier money policy. Four measures in conjunction could achieve these results.

A Congressional Directive to the Federal Reserve Board

At the present time there is great ambiguity as to the responsibility of the Federal Reserve Board with respect to inflation. The Employment Act of 1946 places on the Board (as on other agencies of Government) responsibility to aim its policies at "maximum employment, production and purchasing power." It is generally accepted that there is an implicit directive to maintain price stability. Since the Board does have the powers which could prevent demand inflation but cannot control administrative inflation without creating excessive unemployment, the directive to aim at both employment and price stability involves some measure of contradiction. This contradiction could be removed by a Joint Resolution of the Congress, which would:

1. Distinguish between demand and administrative inflation.
2. Absolve the Federal Reserve Board from responsibility for controlling administrative inflation and reiterate its responsibility for aiming its policies toward achieving high employment and preventing demand inflation.
3. Accept the responsibility of the Congress to find other ways to prevent serious administrative inflation.

Since the Federal Reserve Board is a creature of the Congress, a Joint Resolution would be a command to it. Moreover, a Congressional discussion of such a resolution could be very educational even if the resolution were not passed. Such a discussion alone might be sufficient to clarify the responsibility of the Reserve Board.

With such a clarification of objectives, the Board could

adopt policies which would bring about the expansion in demand required for full employment without demand inflation, while other measures were adopted to prevent serious administrative inflation. The Board already has ample powers to prevent the expansion of demand from becoming excessive and creating demand inflation.

Public Hearings to Check Administrative
Price Increases

There are before Congress several bills which would authorize one Federal agency or another to hold public hearings on any prospective price increase which appeared to threaten economic stability. Enactment of such legislation would provide a check on the tendency to raise prices by administrative discretion. Price and wage controls in peacetime should be regarded as a last resort, to be considered only if other measures have failed. But public hearings on prospective or actual price increases, and where necessary on wage increases, could serve a very useful purpose where there was serious danger that such increases would threaten the stability of the economy and impede economic recovery.

A large number of such hearings would not have to be held in any one year. Authority to hold hearings could be expected to reduce somewhat the enthusiasm for raising prices, and a few important hearings could do much good. The disclosure of relevant data on costs, wages, productivity, etc., would allow the public to discuss on a factual basis the legitimacy of price increases and bring home to those in control in the concentrated industries the policies which would represent responsible behavior toward economic recovery. Such hearings would not be a powerful tool, but rather a valuable aid both in slowing up administrative price increases and in educating the public to the significant issues.

An Anti-Inflation Tax to Reduce Incentives
for Price Increases

The incentive to increase administered prices in order to increase profits could be greatly reduced by a graduated anti-inflation tax. The evidence presented before the Senate Anti-trust and Monopoly Subcommittee makes it clear that the concentrated industries are the chief source of administrative inflation. Therefore an excess profits tax limited to the larger corporations, perhaps those with assets over $100 million, could be effective. Presumably it would only be operative for profits above an ample rate of return on capital and then would take an increasingly large proportion of the excess as the rate of return was higher. Such a tax would reinforce the effect of hearings on specific prices. It is quite possible that these two measures alone would be sufficient, along with the public education involved, to prevent serious administrative inflation while monetary measures were used to expand demand to the extent required for full employment.

An Easier Money Policy

The fourth requirement in this recovery program would be an easier money policy. So long as the Federal Reserve Board thought that it was dealing with a demand inflation, it had reason to pursue a tight money policy. And when its leading economists came to recognize the administrative character of this inflation, the Board faced the dilemma already outlined. But if the Board were relieved of responsibility for combatting administrative inflation and steps were taken to check administrative inflation such as the public price hearings and the anti-inflation tax suggested above, the Board's course would become clear.

How much monetary expansion would be required to support full employment must be a matter of trial and testing which should be left to the discretion of the Board. An expansion sufficient to create the equivalent of an additional four million jobs might require a further increase in the money supply in the magnitude of $8 or $10 billion or a smaller or larger amount. The discretion of the Board should be relied on to prevent excessive demand which would lead to demand inflation.

Of course, an expansion of demand which would re-establish full employment would involve some rise in market prices. If the administered prices were held down, this reflation would bring market prices more nearly into line with administered prices. The resulting rise in the average of prices would be a necessary cost of economic recovery, since the alternative of forcing down administered prices to the necessary extent is impractical. With little rise in administered prices, the necessary reflation might involve as much as a 3 percent rise in the average of wholesale prices, but once recovery was complete, there need be no further rise, provided administrative inflation is prevented.

Such a four-point program could be expected not only to bring the economy fairly quickly to full employment, but to produce a Federal budget surplus of as much as $6 or $8 billion. The income created by the equivalent of a four million increase in jobs would add $6 or $7 billion to the Federal tax revenue, reduce unemployment compensation payments significantly, perhaps by $1 to $2 billion, somewhat reduce the cost of the agricultural program, more than balance the budget as designed by the President, and give a budget surplus of $4 to $5 billion. By reducing interest rates, it would make debt refinancing easier and importantly reduce the cost of carrying the public debt, perhaps by a billion dollars. The Anti-Inflation Tax would also add revenue, perhaps a billion dollars.

Altogether, such a program would increase the welfare of people all over the country and restore the national economy to health and growth. It would produce an appreciable Federal surplus which could be used to finance additional domestic programs, such as school construction, and more foreign aid, or to reduce the national debt or to lower taxes.

The Basic Problem of Administrative Discretion: The Big Corporation and the Modern Economy

The program outlined above is only concerned with the immediate problem of economic recovery to full employment. It is not concerned with the more basic problem created by the pricing discretion of big business and big labor which has shown itself in administrative inflation. Even when administration inflation is overcome, the more basic problem of pricing power will remain. It is a problem which is not likely to be solved quickly or by any simple program. It, like administrative inflation, involves matters which lie outside the framework of traditional economic theory. When an adequate solution is found, the price hearings and anti-inflation tax suggested here may be supplanted or they may become an integral part of such a solution. The more basic problem is raised here partly to indicate the temporary and limited character of the problem and program which has been outlined, and partly to emphasize the need for continued investigation of the role of the big corporation in the modern society.

CHAPTER EIGHT

Legal Implications of Economic Power

The following chapter was originally a lecture given in connection with the dedication of the new Law Building at Ohio State University on April 19, 1960. It carries forward the analysis of the pricing power exercised by big business, points toward a possible solution, and raises some of the legal issues which might be pertinent. The possible solution is extensively elaborated in my Pricing Power and the Public Interest.

I WANT TO discuss here the economic power of our big corporations and suggest some of the economic and legal implications of this power. I am primarily concerned with the problem of the economic power wielded by big unregulated manufacturing enterprise, though what I say may have some relevance to the big regulated enterprises and to big enterprises in distribution and the service industries.

I am strongly in favor of big business and what it can contribute to our society. At the same time, I believe big business has created a power problem for our society which must be resolved if we are to have the full advantages of big business. Also, I want to suggest that this problem lies outside the logic of both traditional economic and traditional legal theory.

In my analysis, I will consider three aspects of the problem: the institutional basis of traditional economic and legal theory; the role of profits and property; and the relation between power and profits. This analysis will give us a basis for considering a new approach to the problem of economic power.

Let us start our analysis of economic institutions with the very simple economic institution, the Ancient Greek family. As all economists are taught, it was the management of the Greek family that gave us the term "economic."[1] The extended Greek family with cousins and aunts, perhaps by dozens, was, in essence, a collective, producing for itself. There was no buying and selling and no market. Within the collective, consumers and workers and owners and managers composed a single entity, and control over the instruments of production lay with this entity, the family. There could be no problem of market price or of economic power as we are considering it today and no problem of its legal implications.

Next consider the institutional basis of Adam Smith's economic theory and the body of law built around it. Adam Smith wrote before the Industrial Revolution had made much headway and the enterprise unit with which he was primarily concerned was the one-man enterprise. When he spoke of labor he was referring not to employees, but to the work of the owner himself. He envisaged a large number of small competing enterprises, so numerous and weak that no one producer had any significant power over price. True, he recognized the existence of government-created monopolies and the tendency of competitors to get together on prices, but he inveighed against both.

There are two things to be noted about Adam Smith's model. First, it involved a separation of *consumers* from control over the instruments of production. The one-man producer was worker-owner-manager all in one and controlled the enterprise. In contrast, the consumer could influence production only through the market and must depend on his influence through the market for the protec-

[1] *Okonomish:* pertaining to the management of a household.—Ed.

tion of his interest. And second, according to Adam Smith, competition in the market would, in most cases, adequately protect the consumer. In such an economy, the main function of the law was to facilitate production by protecting property and enforcing contracts. Some regulation of free enterprise arose in making hostels open to all comers, in outlawing engrossing, and in similar measures. But in the main, the economic and legal theories for the one-man enterprise model were those of laissez-faire.

The Industrial Revolution brought the factory system, which separated the worker as well as the consumer from control over the instruments of production. Control over the enterprise rested with the owner-manager, while the workers, like consumers, could influence production through the market, but had no control over the instruments of production.

Economic and legal theory were slow to take full account of the factory type of enterprise. Economic theory, by treating labor as a commodity and each worker as a one-man enterprise selling labor, was able to retain Adam Smith's model. The only change that had to be made was to include labor as a raw material bought by enterprise like any other raw material. It is true that in nineteenth-century theory, labor became a commodity of special interest and the forces influencing its long-run supply and demand were given special attention. But outside of the followers of Marx, little attention was given in traditional theory to the economic fact that labor was not a commodity.

Also the traditional theory failed to take account of the fact that, under the factory system, a large part of competition was competition among the few. Thus, Alfred Marshall built his analysis on the conception of the representative firm and his industry was a forest of enterprises each having a life cycle comparable to a tree in a forest, growing strong with the vigor of its owner-operator in his prime and declining in his old age.

I cannot go into the economic and legal implications of Marshall's owner-operated factory enterprise as such. What is important here is that it raises important questions of economic power which were never adequately explored by the traditional theorists and which arise in more intense form with the modern corporate enterprise with which we are primarily concerned.

The modern corporation has provided us with still another institutional form of production, one which separates not only consumers and workers, but also the owners from control over the instruments of production. In the typical big corporation, the stockholders have ceased to have significant control over the enterprise. Occasionally a proxy-fight may bring about a palace revolution, though even this is likely to be very infrequent. A recent study of five hundred larger corporations suggests that, on the average, a big corporation would have a proxy fight less often than once every three hundred years. For practical purposes, and most particularly for the purpose of this analysis, we can regard the modern corporation as an enterprise in which control over the instruments of production rests with management, and ownership can as a practical matter influence production only through the market for capital, much as workers can influence production only through the market for labor, and consumers only through the market for products.

The successive separation of consumers, workers and owners from control over the productive enterprise has made it possible to organize production on a scale and with efficiency never before achieved. The separation of consumer from control made it possible for a single enterprise to produce for millions of consumers; the separation of worker from control made it possible for a single enterprise to organize the productive activity of tens or even hundreds of thousands of workers; and the separation of ownership from control made it possible to bring the capital of tens and hundreds of thousands of owners under a single unified control. The result has been the creation of great engines of production of a magnitude, efficiency, and vitality that the Greek family could never envisage, however large it might be, and that would be impossible to one-man enterprise and rarely possible to owner-operated enterprise.

At the same time, in a very real sense these modern engines of production have acquired one of the major characteristics of the Greek family, that of collective enterprise. In them a single management interrelates in a great collective enterprise the capital of many thousands of investors and the labor of many thousands of workers and the wants of many thousands of consumers. These collectives differ from the collective of the Greek family since the same people are not both owner and worker and consumer in a single collective. But they differ even more widely from Adam Smith's one-man enterprise or Marshall's owner-operated representative firm. It is the economic power of these great collective enterprises with which we are concerned and, as we shall see, the problem is basic because collective enterprise does not fit into the traditional legal and economic theories which have been built around the concept of private enterprise.

Central to traditional economic theory is the concept of the drive for profits controlled by competition. This theory showed that when each of a large number of small private enterprises was operated under a drive for profits, competition among them would determine prices and force the individual to serve the public interest. The individual producer did not have to consider the public interest. It was enough if he sought to make more profit. Competition would guide and control his action. And legal theory developed consistent with this economic theory, allowing government to break up monopolies or to regulate them where monopoly was natural. If we had to deal only with small private enterprises, the problem of economic power would not be serious and could undoubtedly be handled under traditional legal theory guided by traditional economic theory.

It is with respect to the big collective enterprise that these theories fail to serve. The first failure is over who should receive the residual profits of collective enterprise, owners or managers. In an owner-operated private enterprise, profits, of course, go to the owners and serve two major functions. First, the prospect of profit induces the owners to risk their capital and, second, the owners' desire for profits induces the owners to operate their enterprises efficiently. But in collective enterprise, these two functions are divided by the separation of ownership and control. The owners supply the capital, but management controls the enterprise and determines its efficiency.

In this situation, traditional legal theory says that the profits belong to the owners. A profit-sharing bonus to management would be legal if it was expected to stimulate more profits than it cost, but bonuses to management at the expense of owners would presumably be outlawed.

On the other hand, traditional economic theory says that residual profits, that is, profits over and above enough to stimulate capital investment, should go to management as an inducement to more efficient operation. According to the logic of this theory the maximum drive for profits would be obtained if the residual profit went to management and only enough profits went to owners to provide the wages of capital. Here we have a clear-cut conflict in theory. Should the residual profits go to the owners, to the management, or whom? In whose interest should the corporation be run? Some say the management holds its powers in trust for the stockholders. This is a legitimate legal inference. Others suggest that management holds its powers in trust for a broader constituency. Few, if any, have suggested that in practice management should run collective enterprise to make the maximum profits for itself. Yet this would be the reasonable solution if, in fact, the public interest could be best served were enterprise run to make the maximum profits.

But here we come to a second failure of traditional theory—the failure of both economic and legal theory to deal adequately with market power in the presence of competition.

Up to a generation ago, economic theory drew a sharp distinction between competition and monopoly. Either an industry was competitive and the benefits of classical competition were presumed to flow, or it was subject to monopoly with results likely to be detrimental to the public interest. Legal theory paralleled this analysis and supported anti-trust laws to break up monopoly where it appeared "unnatural" and supported government regulation where monopoly appeared to be "natural." What both systems of theory failed to recognize is that competition among the few is not likely to produce the results in the public interest which could be expected from competition among the many. Neither economic nor legal theory took account of competition among the few. Conceptually, competition was the classical competition of Adam Smith and Alfred Marshall. And the legal efforts to maintain competition were outstandingly successful in preventing monopoly and outstandingly unsuccessful in maintaining or establishing classical competition. The result is that most of manufacturing industry is today dominated by the "big three" or the "big four" actively competing with each other but with effects quite different from those to be expected from classical competition.

An important break in theory came with the publication in 1933 of Edward Chamberlin's *Theory of Monopolistic Competition* in the United States, and Joan Robinson's *Theory of Imperfect Competition* in England. These two books made it abundantly clear that competition among the few could not be expected to serve the public interest as effectively as classical competition. Where competition was among a few, market forces could not be expected to determine prices but only to limit the range in which prices would be set. And within this range, often fairly wide, there were both an area of discretion within which a price-maker or price-leader could determine price, and an opportunity to make more than competitive profits through the exercise of pricing power. This opened up a whole new area of investigation.

Unfortunately in both of these ground-breaking books, the exploration of the new territory was made with the traditional tools of monopoly analysis. It was assumed that each of the few competitors would seek the price which would maximize his profit just as would a classical monopolist. Further, it was assumed that the price-maker would start with estimates of demand and costs and calculate from these the most profitable price, under various assumptions as to what the few competitors would do. Then the price would be determined by the interaction or interplay of the few competitors using such calculations as background. There are undoubtedly some situations to which this approach applies. But it would seem to be of quite limited application, at least among the really big companies.

Both theory and current empirical evidence support quite a different approach. In the typical big business situation there are two considerations which appear to dominate the administration of prices. First, it is important to a big enterprise that, as far as possible, the minutiae of pricing decisions be delegated to subordinates with only the crucial decisions made by top management. And second, the main consideration in the actual price is not the price which will yield the maximum *profit*, but the price which will keep down new competition and yield the maximum *value*. As we shall see, maximum profit and maximum value are two quite different objectives and each involves quite a different calculus. One is focused on demand and costs; the other on the rates of return which will induce or keep out new competition. In the first, the problem is to determine the *maximum* profit. In the second, the problem is to determine the *optimum* balance between a higher or lower rate of return and a greater or less risk of new competition.

As far as I know, the first logical presentation of this pricing calculus was made, not by an economist, but by a management engineer. In 1924, Donaldson Brown, then with DuPont and later a Vice-President of General Motors, outlined a pricing procedure which is now extensively used by big manufacturing enterprises.

Because this pricing calculus is so different from that derived from monopoly theory and because it opens up a new possibility for corporate management, I want to list the five steps which it involves.

The first step is to determine rate of return on capital which will represent the optimum balance between high returns and the risk of new competition. This is called the target rate of return. General Electric, General Motors and, presumably, DuPont, each appears to use a target rate of 20 percent *after taxes* in their pricing. Union Carbide appears to use 18 percent after taxes, Johns-Manville, 15 percent. US Steel formerly appeared to use 8 percent after taxes, but a few years ago revised its target rate upward considerably. It may now be close to 15 percent. Whatever the basis for selecting the target rate may be, forecasts of cost and demand do not enter into this step in the calculus.

The second step is to adopt a "standard rate of operation" for pricing purposes. This may be the actual average rate of operation over a period of years or a rounded figure close to the actual experience. Thus, if an enterprise finds that in the past, with the ups and downs of business activity, it has operated its plant at close to 80 percent of rated capacity, it is likely to use 80 percent as its standard rate for pricing purposes.

The third step is to estimate the average cost of production per unit, if the enterprise or the particular plant were operated at the standard rate of operation, say 80 percent of capacity.

The fourth step is to figure what price would have to be charged, in the light of these costs, if the target rate of return were to be made when the company or plant operated at the standard rate of operation. This can be called the target price.

It should be noted that up to this point in the pricing process no consideration at all has been given to the demand for the product. Only at the fifth stage is demand introduced into the calculation.

In the fifth step, the market is examined to see what volume of sales could be expected at the target price. If the market survey indicates that, under average market conditions, the sales at the target price will be just about equal to production at the standard rate of operation, then the target price will be adopted as *the* price.

If the market analysis indicates that a larger amount could be sold at the target price, the enterprise will not usually set a higher price since this would produce a rate of return higher than the target rate and attract new entrants. Rather, it will adopt the target price and immediately start expanding its facilities so as to supply the larger demand.

If, on the other hand, the market analysis shows that, under average conditions, demand at the target price will not allow the standard rate of operation, then the management is faced with two alternatives. It can decide not to make the product on the ground that it would not yield the target rate of return, or it can decide to set a lower price and institute a major drive to reduce costs of production of the particular product in order to earn the target rate of return at the lower price.

The sharp contrast between this pricing calculus focused on a target rate of return and the traditional calculus focused on demand and cost must be obvious. Target pricing starts with the target rate of return and works from that to costs and demand. Indeed, as I have said, the target rate may be decided on months or years before it is decided to make a particular product and before its costs or demand could be considered. In contrast, the traditional theory starts with demand and costs. Also, the target calculus involves a balancing of greater or less profit and greater or less risk of new competition. The traditional monopoly calculus, though it involves uncertainties of demand and cost, does not involve this risk factor.

Two further things should be noted about this target pricing procedure. First, it is a great aid in the decentralization of decision-making and thus facilitates the operation of big enterprise. Top management can make the decisions as to the target rate of return and the standard rate of operation, which constitute the first two steps in the target pricing procedure. Once made, these decisions can be applied by subordinates to whole ranges of products, both existing and new. Indeed the final price decisions can be made by subordinates except where demand at the target price is likely to be insufficient. Then top management must make the decision between discontinuing the product or adopting a price below the initial target price.

The second thing to notice is that this pricing procedure makes prices very insensitive to fluctuations in demand. They are arrived at in terms of long-run costs and it is expected only that the target rate of return will be earned on the average over a period of years and not in any one particular year. In a boom year, the enterprise may operate close to 100 percent of capacity and make a much higher rate of return on capital than the target rate. Similarly, in a year of depression, the enterprise may operate at 60 percent of capacity and make a very low rate of return. But the procedure does not call for a change in price because of the high or low demand. Prices may be raised or reduced because of changes in raw material costs and in labor costs, but seldom because of short-run changes in demand.

The target pricing technique may not be rigidly adhered to and different target rates of return may be applied to different lines of product by the some company. It does, however, provide a logical pricing technique and empirical studies have shown that in the United States it is employed by the price leaders in many concentrated industries such as chemicals, automobiles, steel, electrical equipment, construction materials and agricultural implements. It helps to explain the inflexibility of administered prices which has come to be such an important aspect of the American economy.

Of immediate importance for our present discussion is the economic power reflected in target pricing. The purpose in target pricing is to obtain a rate of return above the competitive cost of capital but not so much above the competitive cost as to stimulate new competition. The more difficult it is to enter an industry, the greater the discrepancy between a competitive rate of return on capital and the target rate that can be successfully achieved. A target rate of return of 20 percent after taxes would probably represent more than double the competitive cost of capital. The public utilities whose prices are regulated to allow only six to six and a half percent return have had no difficulty in raising new capital for expansion. Whether the *average* risk in the big manufacturing corporations is greater is open to debate. The big corporation is in many ways equivalent to a combination of smaller companies so that the risks in one division are in some degree offset by those in other divisions and the average risk is less. I strongly suspect that an average return of 8 percent, after taxes, would allow most of the big collective enterprises to raise all the equity capital they need for expansion. Certainly an average rate of earnings very much below 20 percent would be sufficient. Who among us would not invest new funds in a big established enterprise which held out a high probability of averaging 20 percent on our actual investment?

What does this mean from the public point of view? It means that the drive for profits in these great collective enterprises does not serve the public interest. In three important ways the profit objective as the guide to operations conflicts with the public interest.

First, prices result which are above the economic costs of production and profits are above the economic cost of capital. This represents a distortion in income distribution which may or may not be socially important.

Second and more important, this exercise of pricing power aggravates labor-management relations. Excessively high earnings on capital offer a constant target which in a sense justifies pressure from labor for increased wage rates. At the same time the focus on the drive for corporate profits amply justifies labor's adoption of the same drive to get higher wages.

Third, and in my opinion most important of all, a high target rate of return means that the collective enterprise is not making full use of its potential. If a big corporation, despite its great resources of technology and organization and access to capital and labor, will make only those things which will yield a 20 percent return when it can get capital funds for 8 or 10 percent, an economist must say that it is not serving the public interest as it should, or more exactly, as it would have to if it were subject to classical competition. And if a big corporation will replace existing plant and equipment only when the new will make 20 percent on the investment, it will fail to make full use of modern technology. I believe that, in the light of the Russian threat, the biggest cost of the reliance on the profit drive in collective enterprise is this failure to use fully the great potential of big business. From the public point of view, the drive for corporate profits is not a satisfactory guide to the operation of the big collective enterprise.

Some corporate managements have attempted to justify high rates of return on capital on the ground that high profits provide equity capital for expansion and that this is in the public interest. Such is the argument the management of the United States Steel Corporation gave when it raised its target rate of return from 8 percent to a much higher figure. But is it really in the public interest? From the economic point of view, the argument amounts to saying that it is in the public interest for customers to be overcharged so as to supply capital for expansion while the future profits from the new capital go to the credit of stockholders. If the customers were given stock in exchange for the overcharge, the argument might carry some weight, but it does not when the benefits go to owners.

Capital for expansion is important. And insofar as corporate earnings are legitimate, the withholding of these earnings for expansion is legitimate and legitimate profits made on such reinvested earnings appropriately go to the credit of stockholders. But for greater capital expansion the market for securities is an adequate source. The regulated public utilities have raised billions of equity capital for unprecedented expansion in the last decade, while unregulated big business has raised very little. The idea that, for the big collective enterprise, expansion depends on or justifies a rate of profit above that corresponding to the competitive cost of capital does not seem to have a basis in economic logic. Nor can it justify the operation of collective enterprise under the profit drive.

Where, then, does this leave us? On the one hand, the separation of ownership and control has raised the very real question of who should get the residual profits from collective enterprise. On the other hand, the economic power of collective enterprise is such that the drive to make residual profits falls far short of serving the public interest. Can both problems be solved by a fresh approach to the operation of collective enterprise?

From the public point of view, just what do we want from the men who manage our collective enterprises?

First, we want the great engines of production which they operate to be operated efficiently and economically in the production of useful goods. This means that labor and capital and other resources should be combined as economically as possible and the products sold at prices which cover their economic costs. This means that prices must cover the costs of material, labor and capital and that the costs of capital must include both the recovery of capital through depreciation charges and a competitive rate of return on capital. This objective has been spelled out in classical economic theory, not as the objective of an individual enterprise but as the end result to be expected in the operation of an industry of many small units operating under conditions of classical competition and without economic power. Where economic power exists in the big collective enterprise, we want it used in such a way that it achieves much the same end results that made classical competition such a valuable institution where technology made it appropriate. The theory of classical competition can point to the end results that would be in the public interest but not the method that is appropriate to modern technology.

The second thing we want from the management of a big collective enterprise is unbiased arbitration between the parties at interest. By the very nature of the economic power of management, it is in the position of an arbiter, balancing the interest of investor and worker and customer or consumer. In almost any major decision it makes, it can bend that decision in greater or less degree in favor of or against one or more of the parties at interest and with little recourse by a losing party.

The fact of this arbitral role is well expressed in a recent statement by the president of the United States Steel Corporation, Walter F. Munford:

> We of management are responsible to manage the business in accordance with our judgment as to what will best serve the long-term interest of: the employees whose livelihood is dependent upon the Corporation; the stockholders whose invested money provides the tools of production and jobs; the customers who buy our products and thus provide employment; and the people of the consuming public who depend upon steel as one of the basic commodities of modern life.

We have already seen that the drive for profits cannot be expected to achieve the first of these two objectives, that of an economical engine of production. Also, the drive for profits insofar as it activates management through bonuses or otherwise must introduce a bias into its decisions affecting the parties at interest. Who ever heard of giving a bonus to a group of arbiters for favoring one of the parties to the arbitration? Clearly, the drive for corporate profits cannot be expected to serve the public interest in either efficient operation or unbiased arbitration.

What, then, can take the place of the drive for corporate profits? I believe there are two institutional changes which, in combination, would provide an effective alternative.

The first depends on the target techniques of pricing. So far as the mechanics of target pricing are concerned, the actual target rate of return is not important. The pricing process would be essentially the same whether the target rate adopted was 20 percent or 10 percent or 8 percent. If top management found that adequate capital could be obtained from the public market when an average of 8 percent on capital was earned after taxes and if it adopted 8 percent as the target rate, the rest of the pricing process would follow and prices would tend to correspond to average economic costs.

Under given economic conditions a lower price would result in a greater volume of sales and require a greater plant expansion. This would reflect the more effective use of resources. Also, it would give legitimacy to management in its demand that labor be reasonable in its wage demands, a legitimacy that is certainly lacking when management is under a drive to make more profits.

However, while a target rate of return geared to the actual cost of capital would be an effective guide to pricing, it would not provide the other pressures for economical operation which is provided by corporate profits. To find a substitute we must consider the factors which motivate management.

Perhaps the four most important motivations of top corporate management are:

1. The drive for power.
2. The drive for prestige.
3. The satisfaction of a job well done, and
4. The money rewards.

Obviously a big corporation can serve the desire for power, and whether this power will increase or decrease will largely depend on the public attitude toward corporate operation and is not a product of profits as such.

Both prestige and satisfaction with a job well done depend in large measure on the definition of the job itself. If the objective of the game is to make profits, then prestige and satisfaction depend on making profits. But if the objective of the game can be redefined, then prestige and satisfaction in accomplishment need not be tied to corporate profits.

Money rewards to *management* also do not need to be tied to *corporate* profits. Many corporations now have two bonus systems, one for top management that is geared to corporate profits, and the other for lower levels of management that is geared to performance. Under the latter, a plant manager might receive bonuses for cutting costs in his plant or improving product or reducing down time in the operation of his equipment. Modern management engineers have gone a long way in developing measures of performance for executives below the very top and bonuses for performance are regarded as superior to profit sharing bonuses for lower management.

I believe a system for performance bonuses for top management could also be worked out. Such a system would be tied to the setting of target rates of return on the basis of capital costs. It would presumably include bonus payments for cost reduction, product improvement, research and development, and for such other items of good management as could be effectively measured. To some degree it might be effective to make performance bonuses to top management a ratio to performance bonuses earned by lower management. I will not here go into the problems which would be involved in the designing of performance bonuses for top management. For present purposes it will be sufficient to assume that performance bonus systems could be designed and that the management drive for such bonuses would lead to operations more closely in the public interest than operation under the drive for greater corporate profits.

However, there is one problem with respect to bonuses that we do need to consider. This is the effect of income taxes on bonuses.

In the past, most of the big companies have given cash bonuses to top management for increased profits. But with high income tax rates, cash bonuses have very little incentive power. A high-salaried executive is likely to pay most of any cash bonus to the Federal government. If the president of a big company receives $200,000 as salary (more than half already going to the government) a bonus of

$200,000 is likely to net him only $18,000. As a result, many corporations have adopted a stock option plan whereby the top officers are given rights to buy stock from the corporation at the market price prevailing at the time the right is given and good for a period of years. If the stock rises in price and the option is exercised, the gain from the sale of the stock after six months will be taxed as a capital gain. Such options place top management under great pressure to increase profits so as to raise the market value of the stock and obtain income not subject to the very high tax rates.

If cash bonuses for performance are to be substituted for profit bonuses and made effective with top management, changes in tax law would be needed to increase the take-home pay from such bonuses. This I will consider after discussing certain legal problems.

For purposes of legal discussion, let us concede that the economic logic of collective enterprise points to a target rate of return geared to capital costs and performance bonuses to top management. We must then ask, would these two institutional changes be legally feasible?

First consider a voluntary shift on the part of management. Suppose that the management of a corporation deliberately adopted the dual program of a performance bonus system for top management and a policy of target pricing at a rate of say 10 percent when it could average 20 percent. Would this stand up in the courts? I am not a lawyer, but I presume that unless the program were presented for a stockholder vote it would not find legal support. And even if a majority of stockholders approved the program, I imagine that it could be successfully attacked in the courts by a minority as contrary to the stockholders' interest. Perhaps a moderate move in the direction of a lower target rate could be successfully defended by management on the ground that the long-run interest of stockholders would be served. Also, some degree of performance bonus for top management could be adopted provided it was combined with a profit bonus which could be expected to stimulate even greater profits. But for both changes the legal argument in defense would presumably have to be in terms of the stockholder interest. Without new legislation, I would not expect such a shift in emphasis to carry very far.

Next, consider tax legislation which greatly reduced personal income tax rates on performance bonuses paid by collective enterprises if they adopted a legitimate target rate of return closely related to the costs of capital. The legislation might, for instance, treat such bonuses as capital gains. There would be problems of delimiting the corporations which would fall into the class of collective enterprises. I shouldn't think there would be more than 100 or 150 such enterprises at most. Also, there would be the problem of distinguishing performance bonuses from profit bonuses or stock option plans. This I should not expect to be very difficult. At first the line could be leniently drawn and made precise only after operating experience had provided a more solid basis. Finally, there would be the problem of distinguishing between legitimate target rates of return and excessive rates. Here also the initial interpretation could be lenient and gradually sharpened as the actual experience of each particular corporation in raising capital became available. In this respect, I would not be a perfectionist. The difference between a 20 percent return after taxes and 8 percent can have important social consequences, that between 10 and 8 percent would probably be minor.

The real legal question is whether, with such legislation in operation, the adoption of the dual program by management could be overturned in the courts. As I envisage the tax law, it would provide a big inducement to management to adopt the performance bonus system, particularly if the same legislation removed for collective enterprises the capital gains provision associated with stock option bonuses. But it is difficult for me to find any great advantages to the stockholders from the reduced target rate of return and reduced prospective earnings. Therefore, I assume that a stockholder appeal to the courts would be equally successful whether or not there was a change in income tax law.

On what basis can the stockholder be made to have an interest in putting such a dual plan into effect or be forced to accept such a plan?

Here it seems to me we break into new legal ground— or perhaps, as a non-lawyer, I should say here is where I get out beyond my depth. If I have analyzed the economic problem correctly the rates of return on capital are currently too high for the public interest to be fully served because there is neither public regulation nor a close approximation to classical competition. From the public point of view, the stockholders are getting returns out of proportion to their contribution to production and the public problem is to bring these returns down.

One way to do this would be legislation which delineated the class of collective enterprises, denominated them as vested with a public interest and required them to use a target rate of return related to their costs of capital. Such legislation would not be nearly as difficult to police as direct regulation and would give much more freedom of action to the individual enterprise. Also, if a legitimate target rate of return was required, then it would be in the interest of both stockholders and management to adopt a performance bonus plan provided it included a bonus for making the target rate.

The question is then whether such legislation could be successfully defended in the courts. I suppose that the strongest line of defense would be that these collective enterprises are so big that competition does not adequately control their behavior and that they involve the life and property of so many people that they have become vested with a public interest and are therefore subject to regulation, and that the type of regulation involved in the legislation is a mild form indeed. Would it strengthen the legal case to point out that the stockholders had surrendered practical control over the enterprise and therefore were not entitled to more than the wages of capital? Would it strengthen the legal case, if instead of requiring the adoption of a legitimate target rate of return, the stockholders were given a choice of (1) accepting the status of a collective enterprise with all that implies, or (2) breaking the enterprise into smaller units so that it was beneath the size and importance which gave it the vestments of a public interest?

In *The Modern Corporation and Private Property,* Berle and I suggested that the separation of ownership and control made both the logic of property and the logic of profits inapplicable to the modern corporation and that corporate developments "have placed the community in a position to demand that the modern corporation serve not alone the owners or the control but all society." I now suggest that target rates of return based on the cost of capital and suitable bonus plans based on performance would go a long way toward meeting this demand. As an economist I look to the law to make this possible.

CHAPTER NINE

Major Problems in Making an Industrial Economy Function

This essay was given as a lecture before the members of the Institute for International Politics and Economics in Belgrade, Yugoslavia in March, 1961. It followed lectures on the Roosevelt Revolution and on big enterprise and administered prices. It takes up some of the problems of economic management in a modern free enterprise system.

IN THE PREVIOUS chapters I have discussed the problem of pricing power at some length. Chapter 7 makes specific recommendations for dealing with this problem in the immediate future while recovery from low levels of employment is being achieved. Chapter 8 suggests a direction to be explored in providing a permanent solution to the pricing power of the big, modern corporations. This essay takes up three other major problems created by the corporate revolution:

1. The maintenance of full employment without inflation.
2. The achievement of balance in external payment in the presence of inflexible administered prices.
3. The role of economic planning as an aid to stable economic growth.

It must be understood that we have not yet arrived at a definitive solution for these problems. The Roosevelt administration set us in the right direction and made considerable progress during its first few years. But then the war intervened. After the war, the Truman administration made further advances. In the Eisenhower administration some elements sought to turn the clock back. However, the correctness of the new direction was so clear that, instead of reversing the Roosevelt policies, the Eisenhower administration consolidated and in some degree strengthened them. We can expect the Kennedy administration to carry forward the implications of the Roosevelt Revolution vigorously, and perhaps to develop a definitive system of policies appropriate to the effective working of a free enterprise system predominantly composed of big collective enterprises. What I am outlining here is as much an indication of where I believe the logic of modern industry is carrying us as it is a description of generally agreed upon policy.

Full Employment Without Inflation

Let us take first the problem of full employment without inflation. Under the Roosevelt policies, a variety of measures were taken to increase employment, some more and some less successful. In the light of these experiments and study of the new economic reality, thinking tended to converge on fiscal and monetary policies as primary means for maintaining demand and thereby the general level of employment.

Considerable controversy developed, however, over the relative impact on demand of an unbalanced federal budget as against an increase in the money supply. As we have seen, the Keynesian theorists held that an increase in the money supply could affect demand only through a lowering of interest rates which would stimulate investment. The monetary theorists held that an increase in the money supply would increase demand, not only through a possible lowering of the interest rates, but directly as it increased the propensities to consume and invest. This controversy led to considerable confusion in policy.

Immediately after the war the alternative theories received what the physical scientists would refer to as "a crucial test." At a meeting held in Washington under the auspices of the National Bureau of Economic Research in the early fall of 1945, the Keynesians presented forecasts of the employment which they believed would exist in June of 1946. They arrived at these estimates by adding together three sources of demand. First they took the relation between consumption and income in the prewar period and extended it to 1946 to give the normal consumer demand. Then they added to this an amount for the pent-up demand which had developed during the war when many articles such as automobiles and other durable goods were not available. Finally they added the demand for capital goods corresponding to this volume of consumer demand. They reached the conclusion that there would be eight to nine million unemployed by the following June. In these calculations they assumed that the money supply which had more than doubled during the war would have no significant effect because interest rates were already very low.

At the same meeting, I presented the monetary viewpoint, arguing that the huge increase in the money supply would have a direct impact on demand. Taking this monetary factor into account, I estimated that the postwar demand would be so great that unemployment would be in the vicinity of 2.5 million, not 8 to 9 million. Thus, the issue between the Keynesian theory and the monetary theory was sharply drawn. Events supported the monetary theory— unemployment in June 1946 stood at only 2.6 million. From this time forward, the importance of monetary policy as a regulator of demand has been increasingly recognized and the Keynesians' insistence on the primary importance of fiscal policy has declined.

In 1946, Congress formally recognized the responsibility of government for maintaining full employment by passing the Employment Act of 1946, requiring both the Executive Branch and the monetary authorities to use their powers to this end. Under this act, there has gradually evolved the policy of using fiscal measures to damp down fluctuations in demand and using monetary policy as the positive means to sustain the demand necessary for full employment. Such a fiscal policy is achieved by setting the pattern of tax rates and expenditures so that, at full employment, a moderate budget surplus will result. In case of a recession, expenditures, particularly those under Social Security, will tend to increase while tax revenues will decrease so that an unbalance in the budget will develop and stimulate demand. Similarly, in case of inflation, expenditures will tend to drop while revenues go up, creating a larger budget surplus and reducing demand. This damping effect does not correct a recession or an inflation but it tends to limit its extent.

The more easily adjusted monetary policy can then be used to maintain demand closer to the level necessary for full employment and for the expansion in production which the increases in productivity and in the labor force make possible. The Kennedy administration can be expected to use monetary policy as a major instrument toward achieving adequate demand and full employment.

At the present time (March, 1961), we have more than 5.5 millions unemployed, whereas 2 to 2.5 million persons temporarily out of work between jobs or seeking their first job is sufficient to provide adequate flexibility in the economy. This large excess in unemployment has arisen from confusion in policy arising from a failure to understand the character of the inflation since 1953. This inflation was thought to be a product of excess demand and an excessive money supply and so a tight money policy was adopted to limit demand. Since, however, the actual situation was one of administrative inflation and not of excess demand, the contraction of demand created excessive unemployment. It is only recently that this error in diagnosis has been recognized. The Kennedy administration is clear on this point and is now in process of reversing the tight money policy.

With this combination of fiscal and monetary policies, the general task of maintaining full employment can be handled, but there remain two special problems which require attention. The first is that of local pools of unemployment that result from shifts in the use of resources, as in the case of the exhaustion of particular coal mines, or from such an unusually rapid rate of automation that workers released cannot be rapidly absorbed by normal increases in the demand for workers. Under the Kennedy leadership, legislation has been passed to deal directly with this problem, either through bringing industry to the localities where pools of unemployment exist or through the retraining and relocation of workers. As this program succeeds, the level of unemployment needed for flexibility can be progressively reduced.

The second special problem is that of administrative inflation. The most appropriate policies to prevent such inflation are not altogether clear at the present time and the Kennedy administration has set up a commission consisting of leaders from labor, business and the public to make recommendations for preventing it. It seems to be likely that some sort of government agency will be set up, not to control prices, but to watch the prices of basic commodities such as steel and to report to the public the reasonableness or unreasonableness of price increases. Such price inspection could slow up administrative inflation to such an extent that it would be unimportant in the short run, while time would be given for a more extensive study of the long-run problem arising from the pricing power of big enterprise.

The Balance of External Payments

The second basic problem that any industrial society must face is that of the balance of external payments. According to traditional theory, balance could be brought about by shifts in the internal price level of different countries and this was the mechanism relied on under the nineteenth-century gold standard. But where administered prices play a major role, a society cannot bring about adjustment through changes in internal price levels without creating unemployment and distorting the price structure. However, an adequate long-run alternative has not yet been found. Up to a point, measures such as gold movement and shifts in relative interest rates may be capable of maintaining a balance. Changes in exchange rates can be used, but only with danger of harmful speculative effects.

Under ordinary circumstances, this problem is not as important to the United States as to other countries for which external trade represents a larger segment of the economy. But the United States in the last three years has had a strongly adverse balance of payments and has lost a substantial amount of gold. Many people have regarded this drain of gold as a threat to the stability of the American dollar. But this reaction seems to me to grow out of a complete misunderstanding of the current situation.

In my opinion, the transfer of gold from the United States to Europe is one of the best things that could have happened, both from the point of view of the United States and from that of Europe. It is evidence of the final success of the Marshall Plan, which was expected to accomplish three things: (1) to help Europe in reconstructing its war-devastated economy, (2) to prevent adverse balance of external payments from dragging down economic recovery, and finally (3), to create a balance of payments favorable to Europe in order to return to Europe the excess gold held by the United States and thereby strengthen the European currencies.

Now that this transfer has been largely accomplished, the time has come when the outflow should be brought to a halt. This is a technical problem which I believe can be handled without very great difficulty and without any change in the value of the dollar. Many specific measures, no one important in itself, were adopted to encourage the outflow of gold in the earlier period. For example, the limit on the duty-free tourist imports into the United States was raised from one to five hundred dollars and the Government carried home free of charge any automobile purchased in Europe by a soldier or government official. Now these measures are being discontinued or reversed, and many other small measures can be taken to bring about adjustment without a change in exchange rates or the raising of tariffs or the reduction of economic aid to developing countries. In fact, the outflow of gold ceased, at least temporarily, at the end of March 1961.

The longer run problem of balancing payments where prices are inflexible is likely to receive much more intensive analysis outside of the United States because it is more acute for other countries. However, attention is being given to it by some American economists and the United States is working with other countries through the international organizations in seeking a satisfactory long-run solution. Some way must be found for balancing the payments between countries without violent changes of internal price levels.

The Problem of Economic Planning

Now let me come to the problem of economic planning and the role it has played in recent American economic development.

In the early days of the Roosevelt administration, a National Planing Board was established and functioned under various names until it was replaced by the planning agencies for war production. Most of the work of the Planning Board was concerned with partial planning activities involving such matters as water resources, mineral resources, regional development and similar fields of micro-planning. In addition, the Planning Board set up what it called the Industrial Committee, made up of leading economists in the various departments of government, to be concerned with overall economic planning, or what is properly called macro-economic planning. The function of this committee was not to advise the government on specific economic policy but to explore possibilities and to develop techniques for macro-economic planning appropriate to a free enterprise system. I served as a member of the committee and as director of its research.

Early in the activity of this committee, we reached two important conclusions. The first had to do with the character of planning and its relation to decision making. We drew a sharp distinction between what we called "directive planning" and "facilitative planning." We used the term "directive planning" to describe the type of planning which is carried on in Russia. It was our conclusion that in the American economy directive planning had no role to play at the macro-level, though of course individual enterprises and government departments had to carry on directive planning in their specific areas of activity. In contrast to this type of planning, we developed the concept of facilitative planning, a form of macro-planning which did not in itself involve decision making, but was designed to provide a background or framework for the decisions of policy-makers, both those in government and those in the free enterprises. We concluded that facilitative planning could make a major contribution to full employment and economic growth in a free enterprise system.

The second conclusion which we reached was that the problem of maintaining the demand adequate to full employment could be handled through fiscal and monetary policies and that macro-planning could provide a background for such policies.

In our explorations into the planning process, we undertook two major lines of work. The first was a consumer expenditure study. It aimed to discover the ways in which consumers choose to spend their income and the differences in expenditure patterns which arise from such factors as differences in income, family composition, geographical location and degree of urbanization. This type of sampling study is now familiar and is used in many countries.

The second line of investigation involved the creation of production-consumption patterns which would indicate not only how people would spend their money at different levels of activity but what the production and employment requirements would be at these levels. We were particularly concerned with the production-consumption patterns corresponding to full employment.

We started our studies with three economic activities, those of blast furnace operation, cotton spinning and coal mining. For each we obtained information on the physical input and output of every plant in the country and worked out the basic input-output relations. But we soon found that, in order to obtain meaningful relationships, we had to introduce different combinations of prices because the physical relations were themselves in turn largely dependent on price relationships. Thus, in the operation of blast furnaces, the relative amounts of iron ore and of scrap iron used varied with the relative prices of ore and scrap iron. Also the output of iron per furnace and per ton of coke varied with the proportions of ore and scrap used. As a result, we found that the physical relationships could be stated only in terms of specified prices or price relationships.

But when an effort was made to introduce prices as well as physical quantities, the system of equations involved became extremely complex. Mere complexity was not necessarily an insuperable impediment, and with modern computors the large number of factors could undoubtedly now be handled. However, to obtain useful results from the simultaneous solution of a system of input-output-price equations, a geometrically larger number of observations would be required and the available statistical material is rarely adequate to this task. We were, therefore, forced to seek simpler techniques for estimating the relationships between production and consumption.

We found that we could develop useful production-consumption patterns from gross industry figures by disentangling the effects of levels of income and production from the effects of trends of change and sometimes of other factors. Although the patterns obtained by this procedure were crude, they revealed the essential relationships. Thus our production-consumption patterns at full employment indicated, though only approximately, the demand for each major category of product—shoes, steel, gasoline, etc.—at full employment and the manpower necessary for producing the required amounts of each category. As far as I know, this was the first time that anyone had estimated what the pattern of production and consumption would be at full employment in a free enterprise economy.

Our first production-consumption patterns were entirely experimental and their possible uses were not clear. I well remember the occasion on which I presented the results of our exploration to President Roosevelt and my difficulty in answering his first question, "What use are they?"

Actually, at least three important uses have been made of the techniques we developed. Although the planning agency itself came to an end with the war, our methods and results were used in connection with war planning. In so far as military requirements were concerned, the physical input-output type of analysis was used to estimate requirements. The scheduled quantity of tanks, guns and airplanes was broken down into tons of steel, aluminum, copper and other materials. Then civilian demand was estimated according to our procedures and, where the combined requirements exceeded productive capacity, the civilian supply was curtailed. In this way, the production-consumption technique contributed to the planning of the civilian aspect of the wartime economy.

A second use of the production-consumption patterns was by private industry. A number of the large corporations based their postwar plans on the use of such techniques. The General Electric Company, for example, used the technique to estimate the total consumer demand at full employment for different electrical appliances, such as refrigerators and washing machines, and then decided what proportion of this market it would plan to supply.

The third, and perhaps the most interesting use of these techniques, was the transition from the war to a peace economy. Shortly after every great war, the industrial economies have suffered serious depressions. But after World War II the United States avoided such a depression. This was partly due to the high demand for products which I have already discussed, but it was also due in an important degree, to a very special piece of postwar planning by an agency entirely outside of the Federal government.

Before the end of the war, a group of progressive businessmen formed the Committee for Economic Development, whose initial purpose was to facilitate the transition from the war to a peace economy. This group organized smaller committees throughout the country whose members were sent around to question every enterprise in the United States employing ten or more persons. Each enterprise was asked three questions: (1) how many people did you employ in 1939? (2) how many people do you now employ? and (3) how many people do you expect to employ one year after the end of the war? The first two questions could be answered out of records, but the third required considerable forward planning.

When the answers to these questions were tabulated, they indicated that there would be approximately 10 million unemployed one year after the end of the war. This calculation was in no way related to the estimate of 8 to 9 million made by the Keynesian economists on a quite different basis. But it clearly showed that if we were to have full employment, the sights of the business community would have to be raised.

To this end, the Committee for Economic Development asked the Department of Commerce to estimate the demand which could be expected for shoes, steel, gasoline, etc., if there were full employment after the war. The Department did this, using the production-consumption-pattern technique, and the resulting report, "Markets After the War," was circulated to tens of thousands of businessmen throughout the country.

The immediate reaction to these estimates was one of disbelief. A businessman who read that the demand for his product would be 60 percent higher than had ever been produced in the peacetime history of the country would question the reliability of the estimates. However, the Committee worked out a method for dealing with this disbelief. A Committee member would visit a progressive producer, perhaps in the shoe industry, and would say, "I understand that you think our experts have grossly overestimated the postwar demand for shoes. But what would happen to you if they turned out to be right?" The manager might reply, "Well, if they were correct, I would have to build three new plants." The Committee member would then ask, "How much would it cost you to draw up the plans for those three plants and to work out contracts with the machinery suppliers which you would not have to sign until you decided to build the new plants? If you did this you could put the plans and contracts in the files and forget about them. Then when the end of the war comes, if you turn out to be right and the demand is not there, you have only wasted a small amount of money. But if our experts turn out to be right, you can pull those plans out of the file and start immediate construction of the new plants. You will have saved a crucial six to nine months in meeting the demand."

As soon as one producer in an industry had agreed to take this step, a Committee representative could visit other producers and ask the same questions.

I am convinced that this activity greatly increased the speed of the transition from the war to a peace economy. Within months of the end of the war, nearly ten million men had been released from the armed forces and absorbed into industry with no significant increase in the volume of unemployment. Not only was this a remarkable accomplishment, but it suggests that, whenever our present defense expenditure is radically cut, the much smaller transition to a post-defense economy can easily be handled without creating serious unemployment.

While in this particular case facilitative planning was carried on outside of government, this type of planning can be even more useful for government itself. The Council of Economic Advisers, established by the Employment Act of 1946, carried on macroeconomic analysis during the Truman administration and even to some extent under the Eisenhower administration, although the latter was little concerned with this approach. We can reasonably expect that under the Kennedy administration macroeconomic planning will be used both in connection with the maintenance of full employment and as a guide to rapid economic growth and to the better use of resources. Improved techniques will surely be developed, but I have no doubt that facilitative economic planning, in which experts from government and private industry both participate, will play an important role in the future development of the American economy.